A GARDEN OF ONE'S OWN

. . . .

A GARDEN OF ONE'S OWN

. . . .

MAKING AND KEEPING YOUR FLOWER GARDEN

ELSA BAKALAR

PHOTOGRAPHS BY GARY MOTTAU

LINE DRAWINGS BY ELAYNE SEARS

. . . .

WILLIAM MORROW AND COMPANY, INC.

New York

It is the policy of William Morrow and Company, Inc., and its imprints and affiliates, recognizing the importance of preserving what has been written, to print the books we publish on acid-free paper, and we exert our best efforts to that end.

Library of Congress Cataloging-in-Publication Data

Bakalar, Elsa.
    A garden of one's own: making and keeping your
flower garden x/ by Elsa Bakalar: photographs by Gary Mottau; line
drawings by Elayne Sears.
        p.   cm.
    Includes bibliographical references and index.
    ISBN 0-688-12145-4
    1. Flower gardening.   I. Title.
SB405.B2466   1994
635.9—dc20
                                                              93-32867
                                                              CIP

Printed in the United States of America

First Edition

1 2 3 4 5 6 7 8 9 10

BOOK DESIGN BY MM DESIGN 2000, INC./MICHAEL MENDELSOHN

For my husband, Mike

*A*CKNOWLEDGMENTS

. . . .

I want to thank my editor at William Morrow, Adrian Zackheim, who first had the notion that my gardening experiences might make a book. My thanks also to Elizabeth Lawrence and Hugh Howard, whose firm encouragement got a balky horse into the starting gate and off and running.

Gary Mottau lovingly photographed the garden as if it were his own, and Elayne Sears turned mundane suggestions into delightful drawings. Mike Mendelsohn pulled together photographs, text, and spirit with his lovely design. I thank them all for their very considerable part in the book.

I must mention my Heath friend and neighbor Patricia Leuchtman, who some years ago told me to "get on with it." I finally did—in longhand, on yellow sheets of paper which my dear and patient husband turned into clean copy. My affectionate gratitude to them both.

CONTENTS

. . . .

· ·

*I*NTRODUCTION

. . . .

*T*he idea for this book grew out of an unanswered question. It came after an excellent lecture in which the speaker, an outstanding horticulturist, had covered every aspect of gardening. He was leaving the platform to enthusiastic applause when someone near me wailed, "But how do you *start*?"

My intention here is to provide some practical answers for the beginning gardener, and, beyond that, to provide a kind of road map for other gardeners. It's a wonderful journey. The destination—your "dream garden"—is always around the next bend, always receding, and the getting there, even though never quite arriving, is much more than half the fun.

All the photographs in the book are of one garden, my own, and this is to make a point: I can do it, you can do it. The scale of my garden is decidedly human, unintimidating, and—most important—within the reach of a single gardener.

All English people, they say, are born gardeners; it's in their blood. Not necessarily true. As a child, I hated gardening. It was cruel and unusual punishment—something you had to do on the weekend, when your father told you to. There was absolutely nothing interesting out there for me, and the minutes crawled by.

I liked flowers well enough; I liked to lie down and look *into* them at eye level, from a few inches away, but that was not my father's idea of gardening. "You'll never be a gardener," he said. "Suits me," I said, and we left it at that.

I didn't give much thought to gardens at all until years later, after I had crossed the Atlantic and come to live in America. Perhaps it was the glass and concrete of Manhattan that did it. I was living in New York City and working in a forty-fourth floor office in Rockefeller Plaza. Increasingly, as I gazed out of the window, my daydreams were of gardens, green and cool, with great billowing masses of flowers.

My husband and I found a weekend cottage in the northern Berkshires, a two-hundred-mile drive from the city. We had five acres of land and a small pond, at an elevation of eighteen hundred feet, most of it under a formidable growth of hardhack, brambles, and young poplar. Clearing was hard work, and that first year I had only enough ground opened up for a bed of annual flowers. By the next year, I had discovered perennials, and, although my expectations were often unreasonable and not a few of my efforts absurd, a garden began to take shape.

For a while I was engaged in what I now think of as "combative gardening." I had a rock-ridden piece of land that threatened every day to go back to scrubby woodland. Faced with a hillside space that sloped away from the cottage and with nothing but a huge bowl of sky for a background, I longed for some of the spatial constraints so often found in English gardens, where old walls and tall hedges dictate where the paths, shrubs, and flowers should go.

I may be English, but I am an *American* gardener. I've been growing flowers here for more than thirty years—long enough to know that I'd rather be doing that than anything else in the world.

At first, even the word "garden" gave me a bit of trouble. When I told a helpful farmer-neighbor that I wanted a garden he obligingly plowed up a long rectangular piece of ground. He was clearly disgusted and reproachful later that summer to find it full of flowers. "If it was only a posy patch you wanted, you should have told me," he said. I felt diminished. To him, a garden meant vegetables, not flowers. It took me years of hand-digging to reshape the garden along contours more compatible with the landscape.

Gradually, despite mistakes and setbacks, the garden began to take on a life of its own. It pleased me, which was the primary reason for its existence, but it seemed to please my friends and visitors too, and soon I was being asked to "come and have a look" at their gardens. They asked questions; I gave advice. And those souls brave enough to take it were, apparently, pleased with the results. I've "had a look" at many gardens since then. (That's how I slid—sideways—into professional garden designing.)

Sometimes the garden I designed was to make a new house look at home in the landscape; sometimes to provide the owners with all the flowers they had long dreamed of having. Occasionally I was asked to bring back old gardens, their deep flower borders backed by lichened stone walls, but choked now with old tawny daylilies, ferns, and daunting brambles. These were my favorites, for even in the most overgrown borders, spring brought delightful surprises: lily-of-the-valley, bleeding heart, old peonies, and late, tall, dark-eyed phlox—survivors all, and reminders of lovely gardens past.

I talked to the owners and listened to them for hours on end. I found that gardens meant more to them than merely the plants growing in them, for gardens are full of associations, especially for older people. "Oh," one said to me, pointing out a lemon daylily, "My grandmother brought that from the family farm"; of a fragrant white lilac, "We put that bush in when our first son was born"; and, standing before a deep red rose, "That was my husband's favorite flower."

My eyes were constantly being opened to the extraordinary power of gardens, and the strong feelings they aroused in their owners. All the time I'm working in my garden, even in the bleakest of gardening weather, I have a sense—not a picture, but a *sense*—of something beautiful beyond imagining. In November, cleaning up the ruins, the blackened, sodden ruins, of the summer's garden, my vision is not of decay but of next summer's flowers. In gardens, beginnings crowd endings. Out there, cutting out the rattling seed heads of last summer's lilacs, I can see next spring's buds in the axils of branches. And when I look at a beech tree I see shiny pointed buds waiting, ready to push off the brown and brittle leaves that will hang there all winter.

I carry my garden in my mind all through the winter. The very thought is calming; never for a moment do I doubt that everything is there, concealed, waiting for another spring.

Why do I have that garden, and why is it so important to me? An old friend said once that of course I had to have a garden because I had always been "so fond of Nature." Surely, in this most rural part of Massachusetts there was enough Nature to enjoy, yet I still wanted a garden. In what way was it different? I used to tell myself (I've been pondering this question for years, you see) that a garden is one place where, to some degree, we can be in control in a world that seems increasingly disordered and out of control. Possibly, though I am not sure that's the reason. Recently I reduced the explanation to something simpler. I love the colors and miraculous shapes of flowers. I want to make a place for them, a flower garden that I can enter whenever I want to. I enjoy caring for them, from seed to flower to seed again (it is difficult to write these things without sounding like a mawkish greeting card).

I enjoy the physical work in the garden; it's a means to an end and all of it seems important. I can go out there to work in a wretched frame of mind and feel better almost immediately. Every day brings change and new marvels. I experience astonishment, delight, revelation—and always beauty, undemanding beauty. There is nothing to understand but everything to absorb. I hope this book can convey some of my awe at the wonders of a garden that, every season and every month and every day, strike me afresh.

CHAPTER 1

· ·

HOW DO YOU START?

Where to begin with a garden? "Begin at the beginning," says the King, in *Alice in Wonderland*, "and go on until you come to the end; then stop." When it comes to gardening, however, there are two problems with the King's approach: first, there is no "end" to the garden year; second, though more important here, is deciding when the beginning is.

In many gardening books, the seasons provide the organizing principle. Spring certainly looks and feels like the beginning. There are all those green shoots piercing the earth, buds opening on trees, and so on. But that suggests there was nothing going on in the garden until that moment.

For me, a better approach would be to begin in the autumn. September is the ideal month. After looking at other people's gardens all summer, you decide you want a flower garden. You may have anything from a small backyard to an acre or two of overgrown grass, with some ho-hum shrubs and, if you're lucky, a nice tree or two.

You've probably thought about where you want the flower beds, in full sun or partial shade.

If you've just moved into this house, you'll need to watch where the light falls, remembering the seasonal differences in the sun's trajectory across the sky. Fooled by twelve hours of sun in June and July, you can end up in September with barely enough sunlight to open the blooms on the late perennials.

Know where you are on the compass. Parts of your garden, open to the east, are going to make early mornings a joy. Other parts will come into beauty in the setting sun.

This is your chance to provide a good home for the plants you're going to have. Some of the perennials will be there for a long time, and the preparation you do at this stage will be of inestimable benefit in the long haul.

". . . my daydreams were of gardens, green and cool, with billowing masses of flowers . . ."

You'll need to remove the turf and break up the soil thoroughly. If you're starting really small, with a flower bed no bigger, say, than fifteen feet by three feet, then by all means clear it and dig it by hand if you want to. There'll be some advantage to this—you'll get the feel of your soil. But that pleasure will most likely be offset by how much time it takes and how your back feels afterward.

I recommend mechanical tilling for all but postage stamp gardens. Unless you already own a tiller or are planning a sizable vegetable garden, I'd suggest calling a local garden service to come and do it for you. The turned soil, left open to the alternate freezing and thawing and (one hopes) the snows of winter, will break down and will be easy to work in the spring.

*T*HE FIRST WINTER

With the tilling done, you have probably four or five months indoors to prepare for the big push in spring. Put Imagining first. It's an indulgence, so make the most of it while you have time; there'll be precious little opportunity later, once things start up outdoors. Try to turn what you imagine into a simple plan on graph paper (see *Planning Your Garden*, page 25).

All this time you'll be reading garden books, magazines, and columns in local newspapers. Look for a television garden program that you can watch regularly. From all these sources, you'll discover more about your needs and wishes and learn about such practical things as lectures and short courses that you can attend in winter and early spring. You'll send for seed and plant catalogs. They're available earlier and earlier each year, so once you get your name on mailing lists, you'll begin receiving catalogs well before Christmas. Magazines are a good source for catalog listings.

You're now in a "total garden environment," as I once heard it described. And, since like attracts like, you'll come across people with similar interests. Garden friends are a special commodity. Some of them will have established gardens and will be a good source of free plants (of which, more later); others will be at the same stage you are and you can share experiences, good and bad.

The seeds you order will arrive in January or February, some to be sown

". . . never for a moment do I doubt that everything is there, concealed, waiting for another spring."

indoors right away, some to be sown later outdoors (for more about *Growing from Seed*, see page 68). Plants are another matter, and here you have a number of choices. If you decide you must have some of the plants so lushly pictured in a mail-order catalog, you will have to order (and usually pay for them) in winter, though they won't be delivered until the normal planting time in your area.

Local nurseries and garden centers are a good bet when you are starting out. Their plants will be in pots of various sizes, ready to go, and you need not buy them until the time is right to get them into your garden. The people who work in nurseries are often plant enthusiasts and gardeners themselves, who will help you with your selection. Try to be well informed before you visit nurseries and garden centers. Know what you want, and know it by its proper name.

Realize that plants, like people, don't spring into being full grown. Most perennials take several years to reach full growth. During the time it takes for them to grow you will have to make temporary provisions for filling the spaces in the garden by putting in more plants and by using annuals.

By the time the garden area you prepared in the autumn is open and ready, you will be more than ready to start work. So go ahead and treat yourself to the most exciting part of this new garden of yours: Plant!

*T*WO MAINSTAY PLANTS

Most living room plans begin with a couch and chairs, leaving lamps, end tables, cushions, and knickknacks for later. Begin the same way in your garden. Think of plants whose foliage and overall shape will hold up throughout the growing season.

Two such mainstay plants are peonies and gas plants. Few perennials will carry themselves so long and so resolutely, and give a garden such an established look. Not right away, mind you; they won't achieve much size for about three years. But remember—you're the gardener who's doing everything right and in proper order. These have to go in first because they're not plants you move around lightheartedly. While they're growing but still small you can surround them with other plants that are easier to move.

Herbaceous peonies, in my opinion, are miracle plants. They are beautiful at every stage, from the furled red shoots in spring, through extravagantly beautiful flowers in June, to handsome shrublike foliage tinged with autumn colors in

September. More shrub than plant, they provide a solid background for less substantial perennials.

Gas plant (*Dictamnus albus*) with its lustrous lemon-scented leaves, looks like a handsome woody shrub, but it's an herbaceous perennial. Its flowers, white or rose red, are followed by seedpods that flower arrangers would kill for. (Note that the essential peonies, usually ordered by mail from specialist nurseries, arrive in September or October, as dormant roots. Since your garden would not have been ready for them last fall, save space for them and order them this fall.)

A PREVIEW

With these substantial characters in place, you can set about getting the bulk of the plants you want (see *Filling the Beds and Borders*, page 61). You will have your graph paper plan to help you. But let's suppose you can't find it. (Perhaps you didn't make one—you can be only so "perfect," after all.)

Set the plants down on the garden-to-be, still in their pots, in spaces and relationships that look right. And here's my strongest piece of advice so far: Don't agonize. Suppose, when they achieve their size and show flower color, that some of these plants are clearly in the wrong place. What do you do? You move them, of course. They have roots, I know, but they're not chained to the earth's center. This is your garden and you're allowed—no, urged—to experiment, to move them around until they're just where you want them.

After an autumn of soil preparation, a winter of dreaming and planning, and a spring of planting and sowing—comes the summer. But before you get carried away by thoughts of a dazzling flower garden viewed from the comfort of a chaise longue, remind yourself that this is the first summer of your new garden.

Many perennials will still be quite small and, again, keep in mind there will be empty spaces in the bed. Of course, you can go out and buy more perennials; it's always nice to have an excuse to do this. But as a temporary measure, have a look at the annuals offered for sale at your nursery or local farmers' market. You might see some new and very attractive ones that you missed in the seed catalogs. Find out their names and take home a pack of each. Look again at the packets of seed you bought by mail, intending to sow them indoors in late winter. You have nothing to lose now by sowing them directly into the flower bed.

And what about those seed racks everywhere—in the hardware store, the supermarket, even the gas station? Don't resist; give in. You may never have as much empty space again, or be as carefree. All too soon, caution (and thrift) will govern your purchases, but, for now, have fun, try everything.

You'll be busy all summer and, I hope, loving every minute of it. You will be planting and replanting—not everything thrives, even for the most experienced gardener. You will be busy staking, dividing, deadheading, seeding, and weeding. You'll be out there until it's too dark to see, and you'll barely be able to wait for daylight to go and check on everything.

Before long, shadows will be falling across flower beds where there were none before, and you'll know that summer is winding down. Your second autumn in the garden is here but instead of lamenting an end you'll be rejoicing at another beginning.

*L*ESS THAN PERFECT

So much for the ideally planned garden. Now for the not-so-perfect but more often encountered scenario.

It's possible, I suppose, that you are not perfect and your life seems to be running you and not the other way around. So let us imagine that the urge to have a garden strikes you one day in April or even in May. There could be any number of reasons for this. You may have just moved into a house that has a neglected garden; you may have built a house which is now surrounded by not much more than a pile of construction rubble. Or you may simply have looked out of the window at what has passed for a garden for ten years and decided, "*This is it.*"

Summer is a month or two away. Do you have to sit it out, go by the garden commandments and do nothing until fall? Absolutely not. I have some suggestions for a course of action that, while working toward long-term goals, has a short-term program that will reward you quickly enough to keep up your enthusiasm. Not quite instant gratification, but close.

I am reminded of my own first summer in the country. It began, as rental summers often do, on Memorial Day weekend. Did I hunt for a book on soil preparation? Did I lay out a garden plan? I did not. I had a piece of land turned over and I sowed seeds out of every gaudy package of annuals still on the racks. What a glorious hodgepodge it was!

If you're dealing with an old, overgrown garden that's new to you, ask any neighbors who remember it for help in identifying some of the overlarge clumps. Don't dig everything out. The first year you should merely reduce them in size, and fill the resulting space between them with annuals, a mixture of seedling plants and scattered seeds that will take over later in the summer. While you're watching the old plants and deciding what you like and what you don't, the annuals will give you a lift with their exuberant color. By summer's end they die. When fall comes, you can do all those right and proper things.

If it's your own old garden, you already know, or should know what's out there. There's no reason for you to have a garden of ten-foot lilacs that bloom out of sight except from an upstairs bathroom window, and shabby old phlox in one color—the very pink that looks worst next to orange tiger lilies. (Do you wonder why these two have such an affinity for each other in old gardens? Actually, they don't. It's just that they're the only survivors; anything that might take the curse off that color combination has long since given up and departed this life.)

Keep a piece of everything you feel sentimental about. Compost the remainder unless they're on a neighbor's wish list, which is doubtful. Here, too, fill the spaces with annuals, getting them in as early as you can. I suggest annuals because they'll come through the first summer without enriched soil. Cut down whatever you have to in the way of shrubs to give them the sunlight they need. Hold off on perennials until you've had time to improve the soil.

*T*HE WEDDING!

I have left till last the very worst—the scenario that makes strong gardeners turn pale. It's The Wedding. It may be your own child who surprises you with the determination to be married in the garden (the first whiff of interest in the garden in twenty-five years). Or perhaps back in the safety of winter, you generously offered your garden for a friend's wedding. It seemed like a delightful idea back then but a cold, hard look at the garden today suggests that it was madness. This is no time for garden planning in exquisite detail. It's April, and you're up against reality. If you're lucky you have four months, but it may be only three. Heroic measures are called for.

For a start, get going on whatever grass there is. Can it be turned into a lawn in time? Think short-term. Yes, it will be trampled, punctured by high heels, and scuffed by overexcited children. But face the fact that it has to look great only for the first and most formal hour of the wedding. After that it will be covered by people.

Begin now to feed it, water it, and mow it often. Frequent mowing at reasonable height will be your best chance; neglecting it until a few days before and setting the blade low will make any lawn look exactly what it is—scalped. Cut sharp edges around beds and borders next to the grass. It will smarten up the lawn and make an elegant and clean outline to frame the flowers.

Flowers?

Are you going to have flowers? If you decide not to get into any real planting, take a good look at what is out there. If the garden is limited to a few nice trees and some semi-nice shrubs, have them tidied up (short-term again, remember—no radical pruning this spring). Against this background of quiet green and your spiffy, well-fed lawn, consider using strategically placed containers of flowers in white and light pastel colors.

This is a garden book, so I will not be drawn into details better handled by a wedding consultant. One thing I will mention, however: use a soilless mix in the planters. Regular soil when watered will result in pots too heavy to move around.

Now back to the garden and things that grow in it.

If there are established flower beds, tidy them up, reduce the old clumps of perennials to attractive shape and size. With such a short lead time, you don't want to throw out too many things. Even if they're not what you would choose, they'll have the effect of holding down the bed or border so that it won't look like an instant garden trucked in the day before. Now prepare to fill the spaces in between with annuals, mostly started plants but a few direct-sown.

Do you know the colors of the old perennials, and whether they're likely to be in bloom on The Day? You can tone down any "difficult" colors with carefully chosen annuals. Suppose you have an overexuberant perennial that verges on a bright magenta pink. Surround it with the delicate sprays of larkspur (*Consolida ambigua*) or sweet william (*Dianthus barbatus*) in old-fashioned mixed colors. If the wedding is to be later in the summer, petunias and impatiens, in white and pink shades, would last longer.

WHY DO YOU WANT A GARDEN?

Ask yourself why you want a garden. For some, like me, the answer is simple: we love flowers and want a garden full of them, in all their beauty and variety. Yet other people make their gardens for a great many different reasons.

People whose joy is in working in the soil, in feeling in harmony with nature, and sensing every minute their obligation to the planet, will have gardens of a special kind, affirmations of everything they believe in. On a different level, there are gardeners who set out to create beauty governed by order and esthetic discipline. Theirs will be gardens of sophisticated beauty to which we all can repair for inspiration.

To many, a garden is an extension of living space, and their satisfaction will come from giving pleasure to the friends who will be entertained there. Some people garden against great odds; theirs

As early as you can, get out and about and renew or strike up acquaintance with local nurseries. You're going to need a lot of annuals. This is not the time for heavy reds and purples; white, yellow, pink, light blue, and lavender are the colors you need. In April it may be early enough for you to put in an order for what you want. As soon as the weather warms up, you will be able to plant them out and tend them lovingly until the wedding. This will give them time to look established and, in any case, most nurseries would no longer have annuals for sale in July and August.

Don't reject the idea of seeding a few fast-growing annuals directly into the might be a plant in a pot, a window box on a fire escape, a treasured space in a corner of a weedy city lot.

Sometimes there is a strong desire to create and keep something fully expressive of the individual. The creation may be a garden that is easily accepted as beautiful or it may be an expression of individuality so strong that its form is hard to accept. But whether it is a tranquil garden of classic lines or an eccentric backyard of toadstools, gnomes, and colored stones among brilliant flowers, it is giving pleasure to its creator and as such has validity.

Standing in contrast are the dazzling gardens planned not so much for the owner as for neighbors, visitors, and passersby. Certain front gardens come vividly to mind. "Honk if you like my garden," a sign announced as I drove through a neighborhood one day. I honked.

Despite the widely diverse range of goals gardeners set for themselves, the greatest number of them find working in their gardens is a retreat from an all-too-present and demanding world, an antidote to the stress and strain of daily life. My garden is no Camelot. It's often frozen well into spring, buffeted by high winds, soaked by too much rain, or parched from lack of it. It can be too hot in May, too cold in June. Insects chew its leaves, woodchucks eat the flowers, and mice carry off bulbs. But it is full of flowers, which is why I have a garden, and it makes me happy.

Nowhere is it written that the world is made up of two kinds of people: good people, who like to garden; and bad people, who don't. There's absolutely no virtue in gardening if you don't enjoy it. It's not character forming. It won't confer sainthood on you; if gardening isn't a pleasure for you, chances are the work will merely give you a rotten disposition. If you'd rather be golfing or fishing, get a bumper sticker that says so, and forget gardening. Put in a few tough shrubs, and get someone to mow the grass. Slinging a hammock between two trees sends a clear signal; you don't often see a gardener in a hammock.

border. They can make an attractive froth of color in generous amounts and at the same time help to keep you within your budget. Among fast-growing annuals for this purpose, I suggest annual baby's breath (*Gypsophila elegans*), spider flower in white or pink (*Cleome hasslerana* 'Helen Campbell' is a good white), and pink or white *Cosmos bipinnatus*. The 'Sensation' series can reach four or five feet, and would be suitable for the rear of the bed. 'Sonata' is a shorter white, under two feet tall.

For the front of the bed, sweet alyssum (*Lobularia maritima*) is a good choice. It begins to bloom when it is only two inches high and just keeps on keeping on. Annual candytuft (*Iberis umbellata*) also grows very fast and is pretty in a mix of pink, rose, mauve, and white. A small, marvelously long-blooming zinnia, also low enough for the front of the border is *Zinnia angustifolia* (be sure to get the white, not the orange).

If, despite these efforts, you still see a few empty spaces, what do you do? Well, I once begged and borrowed potted plants from friends for just such a situation. There were geraniums, begonias, coleus, caladiums, and, to raise the tone a little, an urn of lily-of-the-Nile (*Agapanthus*). Everything was safely returned the next day. After all, what did Gertrude Jekyll do in August? She sent her gardeners to the greenhouse for pots of anything that would beautify her borders, and what was good enough for Miss Jekyll, I figured, was good enough for me.

Why, you ask, do I write with such feeling about garden weddings? There is nothing like a social function of this kind for making the garden's shortcomings so painfully evident. After a number of years of garden consulting, I finally learned, and, at the initial meeting with a potential client, usually in March or April, I would ask the question: "And when, exactly, is the wedding?" Invariably, my question would be met with surprise and disbelief—"How *did* you know?"

*T*HE FAMILY

I'm going to assume that you want to be reasonable. You stop short of seeing the garden as an all-consuming passion, but neither do you want to see the arrival of the mow-and-spray truck as the high point in your gardening week. After all, there's a whole life to be lived, and many claims on the twenty-four hours in each day, whether they're made by family or friends, by your job, your favorite sport, or your *other* hobby.

Whether the other members of the household care about the garden or not, it's only reasonable to consider their activities and needs before starting on your plan. There are certain facts of life that may prove to be serious stumbling blocks unless you can find a good way to work around them.

Most important, I think, is what your children want to do. When they're little, there's the sandbox. It's quite a mess for a few feet around it but not potentially a threat to the rest of the garden. Don't hope to keep healthy lawn up to this area; better to pave it.

When they're a little older, the children might have a swing, a seesaw, a jungle gym, or, better than this conventional equipment, an open space for construction and play involving tires, boards, Styrofoam, and anything else to make your yard (and that's what it will be at this stage—a yard) indistinguishable from a pre-recycling-era town dump. The more appealing it is to your children, the more appealing it will be to other children also, and for a while you may find yourself running a play school. Before you can turn around, they're teenagers; now you have a basketball net as a permanent fixture and, for good measure, a junk car or two for tinkering.

Easy for me to say; I have no experience dealing with any of this. I feel I discharge my responsibility by drawing your attention to it. The lucky parents with big gardens find plenty of space for this kind of activity. The less fortunate—meaning most people—must do the best they can to save their plants from demolition, or, knowing that their time will come again, grit their teeth and wait for their young to grow up.

*T*HE YEAR-ROUND GARDEN

If, like most Americans, you live in your house year-round, your garden is year-round, too. This situation is about as simple as it gets; the biggest threat your garden may have to face is your annual summer vacation, and there are ways of managing this successfully. You can even abandon this chapter here and go on to the next one.

Being at home year-round, you'll be on the spot to take advantage of whatever good gardening days come along in earliest spring or latest fall. You can work around your job, on a reasonable schedule, on as many weekends as you want to or as are needed, plus some wonderful early mornings or evenings. I can think of something even better: you like to ski or go scuba diving (or anything else that can be done on a winter holiday), so that's when you take your vacation, which means that you can be at home—and in the garden—all through the summer.

*T*HE ABSENT GARDENER'S GARDEN

You could go along like this just fine until one day you decide you're not living in the rural retreat you moved to some years back. It's grown. You are now living in a "neighborhood," and you yearn for real country. Next thing you know, you own a summer cottage in addition to your year-round house. The home garden has to look good while you're there, in spring, fall, and winter. But what's going to happen to it in summer while you're at the lake, the beach, the mountains?

It gets more complicated. You love flowers, but summer is the time for flowers and that's when you're away, so there's no point in planting at home, but perhaps a few annuals around the cottage . . . ? So there you are, gardening in two places miles, even hundreds of miles, apart. As many of us know, "getting away from it all" can turn into "taking it all with you." If you're in this situation, or are soon likely to be, you will have to plan carefully to take it into account.

A Woodland Garden?

One solution I can visualize, for example, is a garden that will be a delight from April to June, that will take care of itself through the hot months of July and August, and will have something to offer in fall when the owner returns. It would be a woodland garden that could be maintained with a reasonable amount of work.

If your garden already has trees, they will provide the strongest elements in it. You might make a lower tier by planting shrubs slightly forward of the trees. Choose shrubs for spring bloom, handsome foliage, or autumn color; you might even find some that will give you all three as *Enkianthus campanulatus* does.

Still further forward, plant spring bulbs, keeping to those that look most natural in a woodland setting. Tulips are not the flowers for this planting, but almost all the narcissus tribe are suitable. As long as the tree roots allow you to work up the soil sufficiently to make a good planting bed for the bulbs, don't worry about shade from the trees. Their branches are still bare when the bulbs bloom, and once the leaf canopy is thick enough to throw shade the ripening bulbs will benefit. Another thing you won't have to worry about is the yellowing foliage. It will have all summer to die down and either turn into a mulch or disappear entirely.

If you come across what I call a dead-loss spot, some corner of the garden that doesn't seem to grow anything well, consider this a heaven-sent opportunity to put in some of the plants that make nuisances of themselves elsewhere. You could just give up, and plant a standard ground cover such as pachysandra, ivy, or myrtle, but wouldn't it be nice to have white flowers illuminate this shady spot? I'm thinking of gooseneck loosestrife (*Lysimachia clethroides*). It's a bit of a menace in flower borders, but here it could colonize and spread to its heart's content. It would be attractive against the shrubs, its white flower spikes all pointing the same way, like the outstretched necks of a flock of geese. Assuming there is lawn in front, regular mowing will keep the loosestrife under control. The little *Phlox stolonifera* usually seen in soft blues and pinks, is available in a pure white, 'Bruce's White,' which would be attractive here. I have clumps of it along the edge of a woodland, where it is exquisite first thing in spring, and hidden by ferns later in the season. It's not called *stolonifera* for nothing; it spreads rapidly from stolons, runners, which is just what you need here.

As time goes on, you will come across more shrubs and shade plants that appeal to you, and between your additions and the plants' growth, you will soon have a woodland scene, descending gracefully by tiers from the height of trees, down through shrubs to colonies of native plants, to ground cover, and, finally, to mown grass. Mowing the grass is about all that's needed in this garden in July and August and that not very often. There are no flowers requiring vigilance against insects, no open beds requiring weeding, and by the time you close up the weekend place and are back home, early fall rain and cooler weather will have greened up the lawn nicely.

All you have to do in the autumn, then, is fuss around the shrubs, a bit of a snip here and a clip there, and enjoy the first sign of color change in the leaves. You can shred some of the fallen leaves and put them on the compost pile, but many can be left where they fall (except on the lawn). Each year, you can plant a few more bulbs.

In early spring, rake off concentrations of leaves, where they might smother emerging bulb shoots. This will be a good time to apply an all-purpose fertilizer (5-10-5 ratio) around the bulb plantings.

As for weeds, there will be some at first, among the shrubs and in the ground covers, but you don't have to worry about them much, except to dig out any deep-rooted perennial weeds like dandelions and dock. A mulch of wood chips under the shrubs will help to suppress weeds.

A Garden in Sun

A shady home garden, as we have noted, can be left pretty well to its own devices over summer. If your garden is in full sun, however, you have to think along altogether different lines. Whatever you do, don't let the sunshine tempt you into planting perennial borders. What's good for your perennial flowers is going to be just as good for weeds, and things can get pretty wild if you're not there to keep an eye on the garden.

You have several options here. One is to decide to make it shady by planting trees; then you can go on to the kind of woodland garden planting already described. A more interesting plan would be to make a large area near the house into a stone patio and surround it with either a low wall or a hedge, using fairly low shrubs, such as barberry (*Berberis thunbergii atropurpurea*), inkberry holly (*Ilex glabra* 'Compacta'), or that old standby, burning bush (*Euonymus alatus* 'Compacta'). The rest of the garden outside the hedge or wall could be lawn.

Even more interesting but involving some maintenance over the summer—or one grand and glorious cleanup at the end of it—would be a garden with a Mediterranean flavor. There could be broad gravel walkways and some raised beds with herbs.

I can't promise you an herb garden that will take care of itself—the formal ones are second only to rock gardens in labor-intensiveness—but I can suggest a few perennial herbs that could survive a summer without you.

An obvious first choice is lavender. Although there are many kinds, some hardier than others, to many people lavender is just lavender—it's purple and it smells good.

The lavenders you are most likely to find in nurseries in the Northeast (for the good reason that they're hardy) are *Lavandula angustifolia* 'Munstead' (that's the name of Gertrude Jekyll's famous but long-gone garden) and, my favorite because of its deep purple color, 'Hidcote'.

Thymes of many varieties will probably be the mainstay of this hot, dry garden. They grow fast and cover the ground quickly but do not reach any great height. They can survive being walked on and, far from resenting it, give off fragrance when crushed.

Cottage pinks would be another good choice. Attractive, with blue-gray foliage, *dianthus* forms low tufts and mats, and gives sweet-smelling, often clove-scented flowers.

The catmints are sturdy, bushy, gray-leaved plants that survive heat and drought well (occasionally, there is one that does not survive cats, who love it and roll in it). The little, mostly blue, flowers are not a principal feature, but the plant's billowing shape looks right in a stone and gravel area.

These are just a few herbs for expediency; you could give yourself a whole winter's pleasure reading about herbs. In fact, you might find yourself so enthralled by their history and lore that you decide to stay at home and make a real herb garden for yourself. There are books galore, an active herb society, and informative periodicals.

A drawback to this sort of garden is that there will be very little to see in spring; many herbs are late in putting out new foliage and the old ones can look quite tired and gray. Don't think for a minute that things are going to look tidy when you get back. Some vigorous work with the shears will be needed; weeds will certainly have moved in on the herbs and there will be a few in the gravel paths.

"Just a Few Flowers . . ."

What about the garden you want at the summer place? It was to satisfy your need for summer-blooming flowers, remember, so there is no call for formal design or permanent features. But it's a great situation in which to indulge your color fantasies. I suggest a few indestructible perennials—for instance, the weedlike yarrow, feverfew, and coneflowers—and lots of annuals.

Buy your annuals started in packs. Deadhead and fertilize lightly for maximum bloom through the summer, and at the end of the season you can walk away from this summer garden without a care in the world. Next spring, you tidy up and do it all over again, perhaps in a totally different color scheme.

That's my recommendation for the garden at the summer place. But I am also willing to bet that that little space for "just a few flowers" expands pretty quickly (by the second year, say).

Now back to planning your year-round garden.

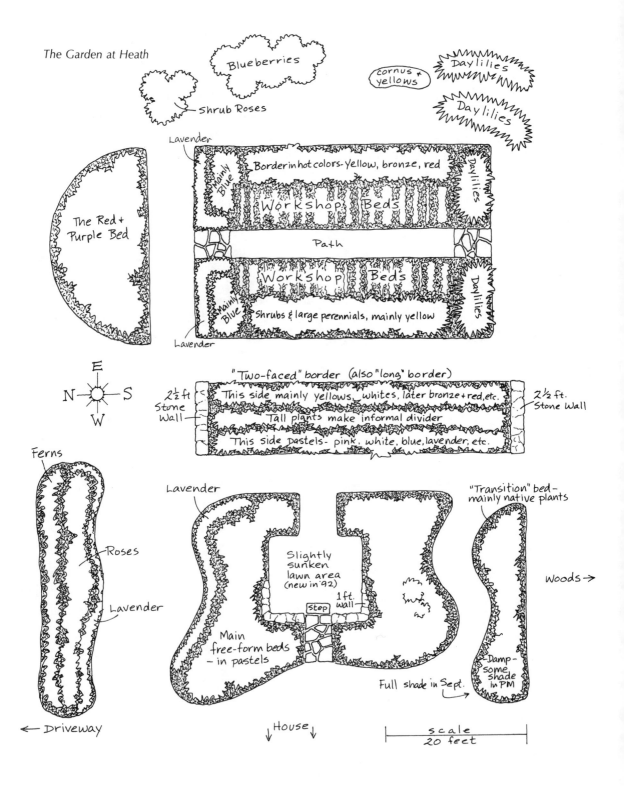

The Garden at Heath

Blueberries

Shrub Roses

cornus + yellows

Day lilies

Day lilies

Lavender

Border in hot colors- Yellow, bronze, red

Mainly Blue

Daylilies

Workshop Beds

The Red + Purple Bed

Path

Workshop Beds

Mainly Blue

Daylilies

Shrubs & large perennials, mainly yellow

Lavender

E
N   S
W

"Two-faced" border (also "long" border)

2½ ft Stone Wall

This side mainly yellows, whites, later bronze+red, etc.

Tall plants make informal divider

This side pastels- pink, white, blue, lavender, etc.

2½ ft. Stone Wall

Ferns

Lavender

"Transition" bed– mainly native plants

Roses

Lavender

Slightly sunken lawn area (new in '92)

1 ft. wall

step

Woods →

Main free-form beds – in pastels

Full shade in Sept. →

Damp- some shade in PM

← Driveway

↓ House ↓

scale
20 feet

CHAPTER 2

. . . .

PLANNING YOUR GARDEN

L et's suppose that you have dreamed your dreams and given your imagination full rein. Now you face reality. I can't know what you're seeing when you look at your garden—or what's going to be your garden. Perhaps it's a long-neglected suburban yard, with a dense mass of overgrown shrubs and weeds from fence to fence. It might be a stretch of countryside with some trees and a distant view, or a bare and muddy expanse of raw soil around a newly built house.

Whatever your situation, now is the time to set down a few imperatives, holding your hopes in the back of your mind for the time being and putting realities first. The realities are the geography and climate of the region (see Plant Hardiness), the size of your property, the local environment, and all the many physical conditions that have bearing on what will grow there. Among those are sun, shade, rain, wind, and soil.

To these realities, I would add one other very important consideration: Who is going to do the work? If it turns out to be you (as it usually does), ask yourself two questions: How much time are you going to be *able* to devote to it? and How much time do you *want* to devote to it? Think carefully about this because it has direct bearing on what you do with your garden.

If you get carried away with too large and involved a garden scheme, you could make yourself really miserable trying to keep up with it. The whole idea is to enjoy, not begrudge, the time you spend gardening. You may get some support from your family and then again you may not. It's much better to assume the work is going to be yours and yours alone, and plan accordingly. This will give you a chance to appear delighted and grateful if and when help is offered, and not feel resentful when it isn't.

PLANT HARDINESS

What gardener, on vacation, seeing something wonderful and new to him, doesn't covet it and then bemoan the fact that it won't grow back home. Gardeners journey to England and come back lamenting the fact that they can't grow gorgeous roses that drape the house like curtains. On the other side of the coin, I have seen British visitors staring glumly at our very ordinary sedum 'Autumn Joy' and muttering, "Never turn that color at home; not enough sun."

Let's face it. Northern gardeners can't have passionflowers twined in their hedges. South Florida is not going to do well with peonies. And gardeners in the Central Plains yearn for the rain and cool nights that make for sturdy perennials in the Northeast. So there it is; you can't have everything. Climate is something you're not going to be able to change no matter how much you complain. We'd best decide to get on with it, and make the most beautiful gardens we can with plants that will live happily in our particular climate.

PUTTING THE PLAN ON PAPER

The standard advice is to plan your garden on paper, starting with a sketch showing the proportions and existing features of the property, and going on to another sketch indicating where you propose putting trees, flower beds, borders, paths. I know there are personal gardens created without this planning stage (mine among them), but if you can discipline yourself to do it, it will certainly help you. For one thing, mistakes made on paper won't cost you so much in either time or money.

. . . .

There's much talk about plant hardiness, which is to say, a plant's ability to stay alive. The first thing that comes to mind is the ability to survive extreme cold. But, equally, for some plants it's heat that can be the killer.

As a new gardener (or one newly transplanted from other climes), the first thing you need to know is the likely range of temperature in the area where you live. Fortunately, help is at hand. The United States Department of Agriculture's plant hardiness zone map divides North America into ten zones on the basis of average minimum temperature, Zone 1 being the coldest (below minus 50°F) and Zone 10, the warmest.

Most of Zones 1 and 2 are in Canada (but not all—ask a Minnesotan). The southern part of Florida and a strip of southern California along the Pacific coast are designated Zone 10.

The USDA's map is good as far as it goes, but any such division into zones of hardiness has to be very broad. The 1990 revision has gone further, dividing each zone into two sections, A and B, each with a five-degree range.

Taken alone, the zones are only a broad guide. They have to be considered along with such other factors as rainfall, heat and humidity, elevation and aspect, wind direction, drainage, and winter snow cover, all of which have direct bearing on plant survival.

For instance, my own garden is in Zone 5-B, on the revised map but it often behaves as if it were in Zone 4. Of course, this garden is at an elevation of eighteen hundred feet; down in the valley, less than twenty-five miles away, it's Zone 6. Even within the five acres of this property, there are microclimates, and I have learned where pockets of either warm or cold air tend to collect. Your own experience and observation over time will give you a lot more to go on.

Begin your garden planning by making a rough sketch with approximate proportions. If you are a meticulous kind of person, draw it to scale on graph paper, but either way don't agonize because you think you can't draw. This is not an art competition, it's a gardener's aid.

If the size of your property makes it reasonable, you can either pace it out or measure, using a long tape measure or a nylon clothesline marked at five- or ten-foot lengths with paint or some other bright marker. Indicate on your sketch the presence of trees, and whether they are deciduous or evergreen, where the sunny and shady areas are, any low-lying damp spots, and the direction of the prevailing winds.

About Those Trees . . .

Are they where you want them? Are there too many for the sunny flower garden you want? Or do you dream of cool shade and want a woodland garden? Whether cutting down or planting more, the question of trees should be settled first. For one thing, removing trees of any size is a job for professionals, which usually involves heavy machinery and considerable disturbance to existing plantings. For another, most trees take their time growing, so the sooner you plant them, the sooner they'll be big enough to add a look of permanence to the garden. While you don't want to have a garden that's a clone of all the neighbors' gardens, it's not a bad idea to look around you; the mature trees that you see have been proven hardy.

The question of trees should be settled first. Are there too many, or do you need more?

. . . and the Wind

I'm a poor one to warn you about what an enemy wind can be to your garden. My New England hillside garden is subjected to strong winds from the southwest in summer and from the northwest in winter. If I had heeded the warnings when I planted my garden, there would have been few plants more than a foot high and no delphiniums at all.

There are reasonable steps that you can take to reduce the problem of wind. Once you find out from your neighbors what the prevailing winds are, summer and winter, do your best to place flower beds where they will have some protection. Years ago, all English children learned poetry by heart, recited it, even. One by John Masefield began, "It's a warm wind, the west wind, full of birds' cries." Once learned, it seems, such bits and pieces are never forgotten. So there I was, in New England, waiting for a warm west wind in winter! Still waiting.

What About Shape?

If the garden area is rectangular, as it so often is, you could take the easy way and make your garden in the shape of the lot, a rectangle within a rectangle, with flower borders around three sides and lawn in the middle. This simple layout is common in small gardens, but if yours is a large area it would result in a big lawn, perhaps more than you want to maintain. Also, the flower borders, to be in proportion, would have to be considerably wider.

If this is not interesting enough for you, then imagine the layout with curves replacing straight lines, the central lawn outlining occasional bays in the border.

Lawn Love

A word here about lawns. They have been getting poor press lately, with much said and written about noisy, gas-driven manicuring machines and dangerous weed- and insect-killing sprays, together with excessive fertilizing and wasteful watering.

Lawn love may have been carried to excess (or so it seems to a flower gardener). Go into any garden center in spring if you need evidence and you'll find fully half the space is taken up with lawn products and paraphernalia. It does give one pause. Nevertheless, it would be a pity if, as a result, we overreacted and had to forego the pleasures of grass. A lawn can do wonderful things for a garden.

The contours of a lawn play an important role in the design, its cool green is a perfect foil for flowers of many colors, and on the social and human level, the very idea of a lawn suggests summer pleasures, safety, comfort, and ease. Not so in China, apparently. A Chinese visitor to England in the 1920s looked at the vast

MEADOW GARDENING, ANYONE?

If you have an acre or more of grass, someone is bound to suggest that you cut out mowing altogether and let the area just turn into a meadow. Unfortunately, that's a trick akin to transforming a pumpkin into a gold coach, for which one needs a fairy godmother.

Although I like the idea of meadow gardening a lot, it would be morally reprehensible of me not to point out a few things here.

Given ample resources (money, mostly), a large area, even as much as three or four acres, could be planted with plugs of established wildflowers and grasses. With a crew to keep it watered after planting, weeded, reseeded each year where necessary, and mown every year in the fall, you could have a meadow worthy of the name. I've seen one done this way, and it was a beautiful sight.

If resources are not ample—or even existent—for creating and maintaining a meadow garden you'd be better advised to experiment on an area absolutely no bigger than twelve hundred square feet (and preferably smaller) because of the work involved.

and velvet lawns and expressed amazement that a civilized person would want such a thing. He went further, saying he felt that grass, "while no doubt pleasing to a cow could hardly engage the intellect of a human being." It hadn't occurred to me that grass was supposed to engage the intellect, but there you are.

I have one strong recommendation: Don't make a lawn that will enslave you. Forget bluegrass and other temperamental species. With a mixture of kinds of

A rough schedule goes something like this:

- Till the ground, wait two to three weeks for weeds to sprout.
- Spray with an herbicide.
- Wait two to three weeks and spray second crop of weeds.
- Wait two weeks.
- Rake, sow seed, tamp down, water until germinated.
- Weed diligently.

(Many gardeners will be unwilling to use any herbicide. An alternative way to kill weeds is to cover the ground with black plastic in the heat of the summer. It looks awful but it works.)

You might well ask why all this emphasis on getting rid of as many weeds as possible before planting, since this is to be a meadow, and meadows are full of weeds anyhow. The answer is that it's a matter of desirable versus undesirable weeds. An excellent book will tell you about this in detail, and I recommend it. *The Wildflower Meadow Book* by Laura C. Martin, published in cooperation with the American Horticultural Society, takes the nonsense out of meadow gardening by unflinchingly telling the reader what hard work it's going to be but what rewards await.

You will see a photograph of my "meadow garden" in the section of color photographs. It's a poor, starved piece of ground sloping down toward the pond. For years it was mown regularly with the rest of the garden lawn. Then one year we missed two mowings in early summer and were rewarded with this display at the end of June.

We now hold off mowing until the waves of pussytoes, fleabane daisies, devil's paintbrush, and ox-eye daisies are over. Soon after that midseason mowing, the black-eyed Susans appear, then small goldenrods and asters, and, recently, the great blue lobelia. The final cleanup mowing is done early in October. I wish I could take credit for this meadow, but I fear I would be found out. So sometimes, you see, neglected grass can turn into a meadow, but not often. I suppose mine is evidence that, occasionally, fairy godmothers do intercede on our behalf.

grasses (and weeds), you'll have a lawn that can be sat on, walked on, and played on. Whatever you inherited in the way of grass can be brought up to acceptable standards and kept decent-looking without an excessive amount of care. Try to find a workable balance.

If you're a real lawn enthusiast, skip the following account of how we made our lawn at Heath (it would pain you).

When we first cleared space for the garden we began with saws, machetes, and clippers. We progressed through several mowers, ruining each in turn, setting the blades a little lower each time we mowed, and in a year we had lawn. Does it have weeds? You bet. I don't enjoy the plantains and dandelions, but I'm very happy with the violets and white clover. It's tough grass and it holds up better than many fancier lawns.

Down the hill, and farther away from the flower plantings, we have pasture grass. We cut it once a year *because grass doesn't stay grass* if you don't. Give it a year, and it's thistles, milkweed, and goldenrod; two years, and it's juniper and hardhack; after that it's weed trees bent on serious colonizing.

Experimenting with Proportion

If your garden space looks enormous, daunting in its openness and lack of boundaries, let me tell you what I've done recently in a two-acre expanse of lawn behind a modern house. I had to reduce both lawn and mowing bills to manageable size.

My tactic was this. First, I allowed the grass to grow quite tall (it only took three weeks); then I had a sweeping curve mown out from the house to make a semicircle.

Seeing how nice that looked against the tall grass left standing behind it, I made a few refinements in the curve and against it opened up a horseshoe-shaped border eight feet deep for shrubs and perennials. This left inside just about the amount I wanted to maintain as lawn. Grass outside the horseshoe border will be mown only twice in the season, and in its relative wildness it serves as an effective transition to the sheep meadow beyond it. Something by way of a transition like this is necessary wherever the cultivated—that is, the unnatural—garden meets the natural landscape.

LAYING OUT A BORDER

In a smaller garden, you can lay out garden hose to mark where you want flower beds, lawns, and paths. It's difficult to see the hose on the ground when you're on the same level, so take a look from various windows in the house. Another technique I've used to help me visualize a border of growing plants involved adding another dimension. My solution was to put five-foot stakes, three feet apart, around the space proposed for the border, and to loop orange surveyor's ribbon over the top of the stakes.

If your garden is set in a wide-open natural landscape, then that landscape itself is already part of your garden; your eyes will make it so. You could block it out, I suppose, but why not use something beautiful when it's given to you? (Perhaps "lent" is the better word, since this is referred to in textbooks as "borrowed landscape.")

If you decide to have hedges or clusters of trees to give some sense of enclosure to your garden, you may find part of the distant view even more pleasing when glimpsed through the frame of a carefully placed break in the hedge. Something partially seen is often more exciting; it concentrates the eye and invites investigation.

Even if your garden is small, with constraints of fences and houses on either side, the same principle of "borrowing" could apply. You might be in luck.

Without room for (or time to wait for) a mature, spreading, flowering crab apple, enjoy a few branches that hang over the neighbor's fence, and let the whole lovely canopy provide you with a background each spring. If the other neighbor should happen to have a handsome hemlock, holly, or other evergreen, you've really got it made; make whatever you plant play off against that dark green form.

If there's anything at all in your garden that would make a background for a flower border, take advantage of it. Before you say there is nothing, run through this list of possibilities: an existing hedge or fence; the house itself; a neighboring house; other buildings, such as a garage, toolshed, outhouse (this is a serious suggestion—a most elegant estate in Pennsylvania has an old one—gussied up, admittedly, but still scarcely a temple or gazebo); a retaining wall of stone or timbers; bordering woods; a pond or pool (water is beautiful but a little difficult to use successfully as a background); a clump of broad-leaved evergreens or ornamental grasses.

If nothing presents itself, as it did not in that two-acre expanse I mentioned earlier, let me tell you how I provided background for the big horseshoe perennial border. Rather than take on the work and expense of putting in a uniform hedge and also, let me say, preferring variety, I turned to small trees and deciduous shrubs. I planted occasional small trees behind the eight-foot border, allowing space for a riding mower to maneuver between trees and border. Carolina silverbell, sourwood, and shadblow, all hardy to Zone 5, have taken well there. I planted single specimens and now realize I must add to them so that there will be a small group of each kind extending back into the meadow. At either end of the bed, I planted weeping hemlock, which effectively terminates and holds down the horseshoe. These are growing well, but very slowly.

Along the rear of the border, I planted groups of shrubs, most of them deciduous, because I like the double bonus of spring flowers and autumn color. *Enkianthus campanulatus* is a favorite of mine. It doesn't seem to have a common name—perhaps if it did it would be grown more often. Small yellow and red bells open in clusters in May, before the leaves appear; the brilliant red autumn foliage is memorable. I am content to grow oak-leaf hydrangea for its huge leaves, the color of cordovan leather in fall, but north of Zone 6 it will rarely give the panicles of pure white bloom pictured in catalogs. *Weigela* contributes flowers in a wide range of color from white to burgundy, while mock orange and many of the viburnum family offer white flowers of great fragrance.

A GARDEN IN THE SHADE

When I lecture, I show lots of pictures of glorious flowers reveling in full sun. Then I feel guilty when a new or a would-be gardener asks if there's *anything* that will grow in shade. The emphasis on "anything" is quite heartrending.

Of course there is, and I'm glad that shade gardening is now getting the attention it deserves. Instead of thinking of shade negatively, as being merely the absence of sunlight, we recognize its special quality of light, and the sense of cool tranquillity and even mystery that it can bring to a garden.

The woodland garden suggested in Chapter 1 (see page 18) was a matter of expediency. That situation called for a shady garden that would not involve a lot of work and that could be left to its own devices in the summer, and still be attractive over the rest of the year when the owners were home. But what about those of you whose gardens are shaded but who want to garden actively throughout the year? You don't want to settle for a sea of pachysandra with an occasional island of impatiens.

There are degrees of shade, with different intensities of light. Begin by deciding the nature of your shade. Full, dense shade such as is found under heavy evergreens won't offer you much beyond whatever ground cover is surviving there. You know what the ground looks like in such places—dark and sour, with gnarled tree roots snaking over the surface. About the best you can hope for is a thick bed of pine or hemlock needles and, for the occasional thrill, something in the fungus department.

If that's what you have, and you can live with it, fine; if you can't, why not remove the tree? Not long ago, at a seminar, it was pointed out that although we are concerned—and rightly so—about the loss of forest and woodland, trees in many home gardens are growing bigger and bigger all the time. In small towns and suburbs, homeowners who began in the fifties and sixties with an open lot or just an existing tree or two look out of their windows today and see big trees, a whole lot of shade, and little else. If they want it, are they to be denied a little more light?

So much for impossible shade (a great place for a hammock—but for someone else, not for the gardener). Let me suppose that the area you want to plant in is in light shade, probably under a deciduous tree with relatively airy foliage that lets light—even some sunlight—filter through. Much will depend on the nature of that tree. So often, the difficulty plants experience comes not so much from the low light level as from competition from tree roots. Some maples in particular, because of their shallow roots, make life for anything else very difficult.

This kind of gardening is a series of experiments to see what will grow. Some experiments may end in disappointment but others will provide marvelous and happy surprises. You must keep reminding yourself that although shade is the obvious problem, other factors such as the type of soil, moisture, and competition for nutrients must be taken into account.

𝒜 CORNER IN LIGHT SHADE

This planting design will suggest how you can get color into a shady corner of the garden. If tree roots look to be a big problem, cut them and sink a metal barrier to keep them from growing back into the area. Work up the soil and add humus, and, if you wish, fertilizer, too.

The plants I've suggested, all being herbaceous perennials, will die down to the roots each fall, so don't expect to see anything in winter except perhaps some leaves on the foxgloves, which are biennial. If you want something with structure that will lend interest in winter, put a few shrubs at the back of the bed.

Consider this design a basic unit, which you can enlarge or reduce, as you wish. Some possibilities:

- Lengthen one of the twelve-foot sides to make a more irregular shape and plant the new area with more of the same perennials.
- Extend each of the straight sides a foot or two and bring the front curve forward. If that brings the bed out into sunshine, then you can edge it with attractively mounded plants that enjoy sun.
- A similar arrangement of the same plants but in greater numbers could be used for a straight border of anything up to twenty feet in length and about three feet wide.
- Among many shrubs that are tolerant of shade and therefore suitable for the rear of this bed are witch hazel, enkianthus, *Pieris japonica*, and mountain laurel (*Kalmia latifolia*) (don't worry—that laurel takes years to grow to any size in the garden). In the rhododendron family, azaleas, either evergreen or

Design for a corner in light shade

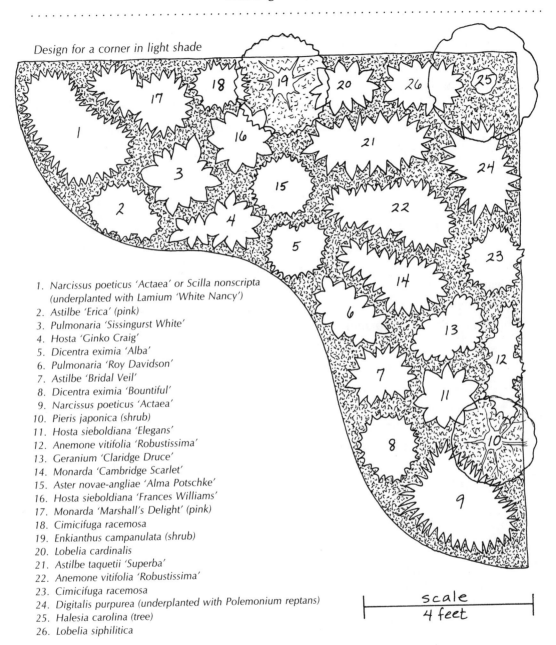

1. Narcissus poeticus 'Actaea' or Scilla nonscripta
   (underplanted with Lamium 'White Nancy')
2. Astilbe 'Erica' (pink)
3. Pulmonaria 'Sissingurst White'
4. Hosta 'Ginko Craig'
5. Dicentra eximia 'Alba'
6. Pulmonaria 'Roy Davidson'
7. Astilbe 'Bridal Veil'
8. Dicentra eximia 'Bountiful'
9. Narcissus poeticus 'Actaea'
10. Pieris japonica (shrub)
11. Hosta sieboldiana 'Elegans'
12. Anemone vitifolia 'Robustissima'
13. Geranium 'Claridge Druce'
14. Monarda 'Cambridge Scarlet'
15. Aster novae-angliae 'Alma Potschke'
16. Hosta sieboldiana 'Frances Williams'
17. Monarda 'Marshall's Delight' (pink)
18. Cimicifuga racemosa
19. Enkianthus campanulata (shrub)
20. Lobelia cardinalis
21. Astilbe taquetii 'Superba'
22. Anemone vitifolia 'Robustissima'
23. Cimicifuga racemosa
24. Digitalis purpurea (underplanted with Polemonium reptans)
25. Halesia carolina (tree)
26. Lobelia siphilitica

scale
4 feet

deciduous, would provide a good background. Two of these, native to northeastern America and both deciduous, are the pink shell azalea (*Rhododendron vaseyi*) and swamp azalea (*Rhododendron viscosum*). Highbush blueberry (*Vaccinium corymbosum*) is another possibility.

- You can even put in an elegant little tree. "What!"—I hear you say— "Create more shade when I've just had to take trees out?" But those trees were big and old, with wicked roots and dense leaf canopy; these are small, almost shrublike, and will lend shape without giving much shade. I have put a Carolina snowbell (*Halesia carolina*) in the corner but a dwarf Japanese maple would do as well.

Now for the herbaceous perennials. My choice is personal and arbitrary, but none of these plants is difficult to grow. I have chosen some for early bloom and some for late, while a few will bloom off and on throughout the summer.

I find white narcissus more effective in shade than yellow, and I prefer the flatcup varieties for their delicacy of form. I think the best of all is one of the very oldest, *Narcissus poeticus* 'Actea', similar to the old 'Pheasant Eye'. It does well in damp shade and is exquisitely fragrant.

The blue flowers of perennial forget-me-not (*Brunnera macrophylla*) look delightful with the white narcissus, and after blooming the big heart-shaped leaves help to conceal the bulbs' yellowing foliage.

For an equivalent spring scene on the other side of the bed, I suggest the traditional English bluebell (*Scilla nonscripta*). After bloom time, the fading foliage will be hidden by the vigorous plants around it.

Wild geranium (*Geranium maculatum*) is a bright pink species that looks light and lively in spring and has leaves that turn an attractive reddish color later in the season.

Lungwort (*Pulmonaria*) is a plant that does more than tolerate shade—it thrives in it. *P. angustifolia*, with blue flowers and dull green leaves, is the most commonly grown but cultivars of *P. saccharata*, most with silver-splattered leaves, are especially lovely in light shade. Look for 'Mrs. Moon' (pink flowers) and 'Sissinghurst White'.

Foxgloves (*Digitalis purpurea*) in white and rose shades are among the first of the tall spire plants of the season. Jacob's ladder (*Polemonium reptans*) makes a carpet of soft blue beneath them.

There is nothing to stop you putting in a big old-fashioned bleeding heart (*Dicentra spectabilis*) in a shade border. Just remember that it dries up, browns, and goes dormant for the summer, leaving a large hole. This is why *D. eximia* is a much better choice for this bed. It has a smaller plant with attractive ferny foliage and it blooms intermittently through the summer. A number of named cultivars like 'Bountiful' and 'Luxuriant' give you choice of color.

There are hostas in any size you fancy; choose a small variety for the front, and go all out on a big-leafed one further back (you may be surprised at how much of the bed this can take up).

A low white astilbe (*Astilbe arendsii* 'Bridal Veil') will pair well with pink *Dicentra eximia* toward the front of the bed. A tall, late astilbe in a rose-purple shade (*Astilbe taquetii* 'Superba') will be a good companion for the blue lobelia (*Lobelia siphilitica*), which blooms later than the scarlet cardinal flower (*L. cardinalis*).

Put the bee balm (*Monarda didyma*) where it gets more light than the other plants; it will bloom but, without sunlight, none too generously. I suggest a light red such as 'Cambridge Scarlet'. Near it, the tall white wands of snakeroot (*Cimicifuga racemosa*) will be in effective contrast.

For late summer, asters offer a wide choice but they present some problems in shade, so I have suggested only one, *Aster novae-angliae* 'Alma Potschke'. If it's not too shaded, its glowing rose-red flowers will more than repay you for the gamble.

Japanese anemone will be among the last to bloom, but its grapeleaf foliage will be handsome all summer. *Anemone vitifolia* 'Robustissima' is the easiest one of the tribe to grow, and usually comes into bloom safely ahead of the first frost.

Don't forget hardy ferns, so useful for filling in when flowering perennials are resting, and ground covers such as wild ginger (*Asarum canadensis*) or *Lamium* 'White Nancy'.

In the first year, while perennials are relatively small, you may have spaces to fill. No need to repeat here that, in general, annuals are not for shade. Among the few exceptions is impatiens, that good-natured plant that takes sun or shade. But rather than resorting to this and nothing else, slip in a few pansies, keeping to light colors, white and pale blue giving the best effect. Make your own experiments with any annuals that are said to tolerate shade, such as monkey flower (*Mimulus*) and wishbone flower (*Torenia*). If all else fails, drop in a potted tuberous begonia. All's fair in a shady corner!

CHAPTER 3

. . . .

GARDENING FROM THE GROUND UP

"*P*laying in the dirt, I see," someone once remarked on seeing me working in the garden. That "dirt," in a layer only a few inches deep in places, provides sustenance for our entire planet. Forget the word dirt; let's call it earth or soil.

A prize rosebush in a garden, a geranium in a window box, a dandelion in a sidewalk crack—all of them have put down roots and are making the best of the soil they find there. Plants are extraordinarily adaptable, and most will grow or at least survive in soil that is far from perfect.

But I know you want the best for the plants you're looking forward to growing in this garden of yours, so let's start by looking at the makeup of a good soil. It should drain well but hold sufficient moisture for the plants' needs. It will do this if there is a good balance between sand and clay.

For general purposes it should be neither excessively acid nor excessively alkaline. The topsoil should be fertile, loose, and well aerated; subsoil should not be compacted into nondraining "hardpan."

You might have the good fortune to take over a garden whose previous owner has spent a lifetime working to this end. But, at the other extreme, you might be facing a particularly bad situation. If you have bought or built a new house, for example, and the lot looks as if it had been scraped down to subsoil, it probably has. In that case, you may have to take the radical and expensive step of replacing it with quantities of good quality topsoil. For all situations in between these extremes, you must check out the soil.

*T*HE pH FACTOR

It sounds like the title of a whodunit, but the pH factor (that's right—small p, big H) is a measure of the soil's acidity, on a scale of 1 (most acid) to 14 (most alkaline).

As a rule of thumb, gardeners east of the Mississippi are likely to have acid soil; those west of the Mississippi alkaline soil. To find out the pH of your soil you can send samples away for testing or buy an inexpensive home kit and do it yourself. With a reading between 5.5 and 7, you can grow just about anything you want to in the way of flowers.

The usual recommendation for excessively acid soil is to add limestone, which makes the nutrients in the soil more accessible to plants. For excessively alkaline soil, the remedy is to add sulfur.

Ideally, I suppose, we should take what nature gives us and grow what comes naturally. But gardeners—being, as I've said before, a greedy lot—always want something they don't have.

I have to tell you here that in my home garden, if everything is growing well, with good foliage and flowers, I leave it alone on the old but valid theory that "if it ain't broke, don't fix it."

*S*ANDY SOIL AND CLAY SOIL

First take the evident indications—what you can see and feel. Heavy clay soil is immediately apparent (on your boots, for instance). Test by taking up and pressing a handful; it will hold together in a sticky mass. Clay soil drains poorly, stays cold well into spring (making early planting difficult), and dries into hard lumps and clods in summer.

At the other end of the scale, and just as evident a problem, is soil that is too sandy. The particles are large and coarse, as you can feel in your hand. This soil won't hold together under pressure, but sifts through your fingers. It does not retain moisture, and nutrients leach from it quickly.

Interestingly enough, humus is an important part of the remedy for both of these problem soils. The addition of generous amounts of organic matter such as compost or manure helps to unite the small particles of clay soil into larger units, improving drainage and aeration, while the same materials added to excessively sandy soil increase that soil's ability to hold water and nutrients.

Humus, a general term for decayed vegetable or animal matter, is essential in the makeup of a good soil, but is often present in insufficient quantity. Animal manure has been used for centuries, and its virtues are well-known, but it is getting more difficult to come by and substitutes must often be used. The actual nutritional value of many kinds of organic matter may not be very high, but the improvement that it brings about in the texture, or *tilth*, of the soil is unquestionably great. This, in turn, means that the soil can hold on to moisture and nutrients long enough to benefit the plants.

Growing a cover crop and turning or tilling it in is another way to improve poor soil. One disadvantage to this "green manuring," as it is often called, is the time it takes. If you are able to plan in advance, sow spring oats in August. They will be killed by frost late in the year but will break down and provide humus in the soil. This schedule has the advantage of not wasting any of the growing season.

If you don't have a winter in which to prepare, you can sow buckwheat after the last frost in spring. It is fast-growing and can be turned in after about four weeks, giving you time to plant a garden by approximately the end of June.

COMPOST

Today the buzz word is compost. Composting involves piling layers of materials such as leaves, weeds, kitchen waste, lawn clippings, manure, spent plants, and a little soil, in such a way that they decompose into humus.

A compost pile may be just that—a pile of garden rubbish dumped behind a convenient hedge to get it out of the way. Discovered a year or two later, it turns out to have decayed and crumbled into a dark rich humus ready to be used in the garden. Accidental compost, you might say.

Rather than waiting for accidental composting, however, a thrifty gardener will set up a system that will yield a steady supply of compost. At the same time it disposes of all manner of waste that would otherwise be clogging landfills.

Kitchen waste is an important element in the home gardener's composting program. What a good use for such things as spoiled greens, vegetable and fruit peelings, tea leaves, coffee grounds, eggshells, and all those good things that used to be put out to be carted away and incinerated!

There are some things that should not be put on the compost pile: fat, oil, or grease in quantity; dog or human feces; all of the contents of cat litter boxes.

Furthermore, unless you're planning an all-night snack bar for raccoons and other so-called varmints, don't put meat and fish scraps on the pile. They have value, all right, and are used in big commercial composting operations, but they should not be used in small suburban yards where they could offend neighbors.

As more and more gardeners come to recognize the value of compost they look further afield for materials to add to their home supply. "Taking out the garbage" may become "bringing in the garbage." In a recent exhaustive survey of composting techniques, Rodale Press suggests that you might strike a deal with your local pet store—you get the cage litter, bird droppings, and all, in exchange for cleaning out the bird cages. Now there's a thought . . .

You can be as plain or as fancy as you like in your composting. I've seen catalogs with as many as four pages devoted to composting equipment. I must say I cringe a bit when, after all my talk about compost, students ask to see my composting setup. It's a rudimentary framework of chicken wire stapled to old timbers and a few metal posts. It's not that I wouldn't like to have a good-looking, scientific compost bin—it's just that I started with an improvisation and it still works, so a replacement is fairly low on my list of wants.

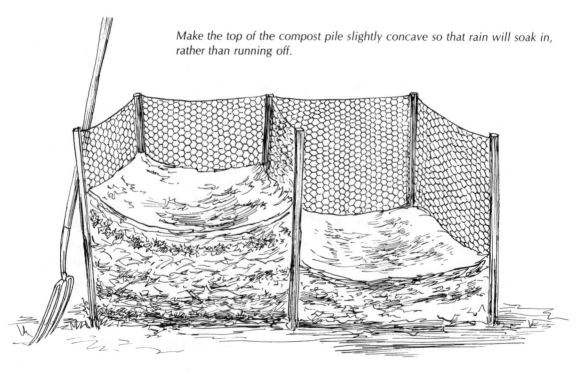

Make the top of the compost pile slightly concave so that rain will soak in, rather than running off.

My setup gives me a large bin with two sections, open to the front. The vegetable matter goes into one section in layers until the pile is about four feet high. In summer, the warmth accelerates the decomposition process and, in a few weeks, I turn the pile over into the other section so that the top—the least decomposed part—becomes the bottom. Now I can start a new pile in the first section of the bin.

My compost area is in partial shade, hidden from the house by shrubbery and reached by a path wide enough for a large garden cart. I chose the site for esthetic reasons, but I do wish it were not so sharply uphill from every part of the garden. A cartload of plant material and damp soil is heavy and the temptation to pitch it over the wall is very strong. Put yours where you can get to it easily, or you won't use it as often as you should.

In my part of the world there is little or no decomposition in the cold months of winter (I sometimes find the center of the compost pile still frozen solid in early May). Because my system is a bit haphazard, the internal temperature of the pile is not high enough to destroy weed seeds. I can just imagine the proliferation of weeds if I were to do what is often recommended and spread it on top of the ground like a mulch. I put my compost underground, where it works wonders.

Using the Compost

Each spring, I buy a good many one-year-old perennials and line them out in the production garden. I want them to grow quickly but not at the expense of strength. At this stage they are small, with modest root systems and, since they will be in this first location for only a month or so, I can plant them quite close together. I line the bottom of each hole with a trowelful of compost, put a little soil on top of that, and set the young plant on it. I know for a certainty that because of that compost the plants will make rapid and strong growth, starting with the roots.

I like my garden students to check out the progress for themselves. I enjoy seeing their amazement when they dig up these little perennials that they had planted only two or three weeks before. They see the remarkable root systems that have developed, with threadlike feeder roots penetrating and clinging to the fibrous compost. Seeing is believing.

Compost goes at the bottom of the hole, to hold moisture and provide nourishment for the roots of a young transplant.

I use compost for every single planting operation throughout the season. In fact, I make it a rule that not only should compost be at the bottom of any hole a plant is going into, but the hole it left behind should be filled with compost, too. And since, in a teaching garden, plants are moved frequently, this practice helps maintain the level and fertility of soil in the flower beds.

I'm not alone in this enthusiasm for compost. A friend of mine who had just sold her house understood, quite rightly, that the garden and all its plants would remain. "But," she said vehemently, "they're not getting the compost!" And they didn't; she bagged it and took it with her. I fully expect to find in the newspaper one day that custody of the compost is a burning issue in some divorce settlement.

Working with the Soil

In the thirty years since I've had my hillside garden there has been an enormous change in the way all of us, and not just gardeners, think about the planet we inhabit. As a result, there's more sophistication to the efforts of even a rank beginner than there was when I started. Make no mistake about it; I was a rank beginner, all right. The few scraps of gardening "knowledge" I thought I had were what I must have absorbed, however unconsciously, from my gardening family in England many years before. All I wanted to do was grow something, and as soon as the neighboring farmer had opened up that strip of land for me, I was out there with my seeds.

I remember sunflowers, poppies, and marigolds that bloomed well, but I also remember carrots that grew only a few inches and stopped, making hardly any growth at all underground. I recall my farmer friend telling me I would have to "work up the soil," and another neighbor's reference to something she called "humus," without which, she said, I wouldn't have any luck with vegetables or perennial flowers. I didn't listen that first year, but I soon found out what they were trying, ever so gently, to tell me.

This is not a treatise on the science of composting or soil improvement in general. There are many excellent books, some of them lively and entertaining reading. All I hope to do here is share with you the enjoyment to be had in working with soil, getting the feel of it, adding to it, and watching it improve, not just for immediate pleasure, but for the sense of doing something as a good steward of the land.

This is all very well, you're thinking, but here I am looking at something close to a disaster area and wondering where to start. I know it's a daunting sight—a piece of land left untended for a season or longer. Whether it's an old and overgrown garden, a neglected pasture, or a long-empty suburban lot that's been taken over by weeds and worse, you can make your life easier by tackling the problem in logical stages.

First, cut down whatever is growing there as close to soil level as you can. You may do this with a big mower, a weed whacker, a field and brush mower, a scythe—it all depends on the size of what's growing there, the amount of space you have to work in, and available labor. ("Available labor" really means, "Who's going to do it?") Whatever machine is used, rake up as much as you can.

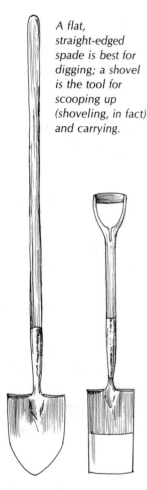

A flat, straight-edged spade is best for digging; a shovel is the tool for scooping up (shoveling, in fact) and carrying.

You may think that the next stage, the tilling, will take care of what sod remains, but in my experience it doesn't. Few home garden tillers can break up those fibrous root masses enough to prevent their growing again, and I'm sure you don't want to spend the next year or so digging out sprouting roots. Use the sods (grass side down) to outline an area for a compost pile, or stack them in some out-of-the-way place, where they can be left to break down slowly into compost.

If you're preparing flower beds of manageable size, I recommend hand-digging. You will hear a lot about something called double digging, but not here, though I've done it, and I know it's a wonderful way to provide plants with a deeper-than-usual layer of topsoil. It is said that it will double the life of the garden, but it also may halve the life of the gardener.

Like any other job, digging is a breeze if you use the right tools. Don't try to dig with a shovel. A shovel is a rounded tool designed to scoop up and carry things like sand or manure. A spade has a flat edge. You aren't planning to carry that soil anywhere, but merely to turn it upside down. You wouldn't try to cut an apple with a teaspoon; you'd use something with a knife edge, so use a spade.

I enjoy digging. I find out a lot about the soil as I dig. I remove large stones, dig out the taproots of obstinate weeds, and take note of the activity of below-ground creatures. Often I discover how different soils are from one part of the garden to the next. This information is invaluable when choosing the right place for a plant.

If you have a year's lead time, October is the ideal month for digging. Clear skies, cooler temperatures, and no insects make it a pleasure. If your soil has been tested and found to be too acid, this is an excellent time to apply lime. It should be spread on top and allowed to work its way into the open soil over winter.

This is the only time it is safe to leave soil open. Normally, you'd sow a cover crop. Annual weeds don't grow in winter, but the seeds are right there, as they will be for years, ready, willing, and able. And they can beat you to it in spring if you're not quick.

After the winter cycles of freezing and thawing, the soil should be crumbly, well-aerated and, once it dries out sufficiently, ready for planting. I can't overemphasize the importance of waiting for the soil to dry.

To keep you out of trouble while you're waiting, you might take a look at some established flower gardens in your neighborhood. From them you can learn a lot about what to expect in your own garden. Whatever is up and growing has come safely through the winter and must be pretty hardy. While your neighbor is showing you the garden, admire what you see and like—it may be a large plant that's due for division, in which case you could be in luck.

Lest you think I'm suggesting that gardeners become nothing more than scroungers, Chapter 5 is devoted to the many (honorable) ways of obtaining the plants to fill your garden. But first—a look at a gardener's life in the delirious days of spring.

CHAPTER 4

. . . .

YOUR GARDEN IN SPRING

*T*here comes that wonderful day in spring—early some years, later in others—when I first go out into the garden. There may be snow still under the hedges and against the stone walls, but it's gone from the garden. I can see the first signs of growth from the perennials, perhaps a sharp chartreuse or soft blue-green. That's all it takes, the merest suggestion of color against the dark damp earth, and another gardening year has begun for me.

To look at a cluster of curled blue-green leaves, one inch out of the ground, is enough for me to envision an airy meadow rue, its sulfur yellow flowers reaching to eye level. Tiny pale yellow spears promise iris in rainbow colors. The shell of a poppy seed head from last summer, so skeletonized by winter weather as to look like a minute bird cage, recalls the lush satin flowers of June. Today, everything is promising, everything is possible.

Such imaginings are all very well, but gardens are not made in the mind. So, I tell myself to get on with it. Almost immediately I remember my own advice: *Keep off that soft, newly thawed soil.* I decide to listen to it, and resume my examination of the relics of last year's garden.

Just looking at the soil, I can put together in my mind what has gone on there over the past four or five months. We leave the summer house and garden at the end of October (or early in November if the autumn arrives gently) and don't usually get back up there until mid-April. In a good winter snow comes early and, except for one late winter thaw, remains on the ground, insulating the plants. In spring, with the last of the snow melting, and the frost releasing its grip on the earth, the garden runs with water.

Daily thawing and nightly freezing may be great for maple sugaring but it makes a mess of the garden. Tubes of soil are forced up three or four inches and frozen on the surface. Often these frozen cylinders carry small plants up with them. One look at this scene suggests an immediate planting rule for this and other areas where the spring arrives in fits and starts. Don't plant perennials in fall unless they will have time to make good growth before winter.

At this time of year in New England, nobody gets more fidgety than a gardener. It's asking too much of a body not to rush out and plant something, even in mud, but another rule offers itself here: hold on. On that first day, the surface of the soil has drained a little (it now looks like oatmeal) but, as I know from experience, one step and it will fill your boots or shoes. The damage you should worry about is not a boot full of water, however, but what you would be doing to the soil in its vulnerable condition. The consequences (other than a deep hole rapidly filling with water) won't be immediately visible, but just wait until that compacted mud dries into clay. You will barely be able to break up the clods with a spade.

What one has to do is wait until everything is thoroughly drained and a combination of spring sun and wind dries the soil to acceptable planting condition. Leaving the soil alone will allow this to happen. In the meantime, there's no need to sit down and twiddle your thumbs; there are plenty of jobs to keep you out of trouble while things dry out. For instance:

- Can you lay your hands on last year's notebook in which you wrote all your reminders for this spring?
- We'll assume you have put in your mail orders. Now scout out the local nurseries to see what's available this year.
- Buy some dahlia tubers while the selection is good. If you have your own tubers in storage, check to see that they're neither too dry nor wet; if they have begun to sprout, pot them up and keep them in a cool place. They don't go out in the ground until danger of frost is past. Do you know your average last frost date?
- Check your supplies of fertilizer, peat moss, Jiffy-Mix, or other sterile starter mix, for seeding.
- Look around to see what mulch material is available for trees and shrubs at the nursery and other local sources.
- What about the garden tools, hose lengths and connections? The tools should have had a good cleaning before they were put away for winter.

Perhaps they did; if not, clean them now. You can sandpaper away any roughness on wooden handles and apply a coat of clear shellac to preserve the wood and save you from splinters.

- Treat yourself to one more good tool—you're going to deserve it.
- Where are the seeds you saved from last year? How many are viable? (See *Growing from Seed*, page 68.)
- Organize this year's seed packets in order of planting.
- Do you have labels ready, and a marking pen?
- Have you checked your compost pile? If you don't have one yet then this is the time to start one (See *Compost*, page 43). With temperatures of 50° Fahrenheit and above, you could start on the first turning of the pile. If yours is anything like mine is in early April, you might be able to fork off the top six inches or so before striking solid ice.
- Gather together in one place stakes, brush, and other plant supports. Have ready a few tomato cages or similar devices to hold up baby's breath, ground clematis, and other such sprawlers. Buy twine in a neutral color, *not emerald green!*

The number of things you can do is nearly endless, and most of them seem unattractive to someone who only wants to get out and garden. In fact, I can scarcely bear to list any more here, but this is the time for lists and resolution. At such a busy time priorities are important, so make yourself a list—several lists if need be. If your work day goes the way mine often does, you might get the first two or three jobs done. My father, that resolute man, made a list every night of things he was to do next day. Usually, he put down about twenty items and was able to reach number fifteen at least. Number one on the list was always "Get up." I asked him about it. "On a really bad day," he said, "that's one thing I can check off."

Even if the soil looks fine, I suggest you try the standard test before getting out there on it. Pick up a handful of soil and squeeze it. If it holds together briefly in a soft ball and soon crumbles apart, it's ready to work with. If it makes a solid, doughlike ball and holds together, keep off the garden for a few more days. I make one exception to the keep-off rule. After violent fluctuation in temperature, plants may be heaved up out of the ground. Press them back down gently. Stand on a wide board to avoid sinking and compacting the earth. And keep the board at hand, as you will need it again and again.

Looking out of the window during this waiting stage, the thing I find astonishing is how one day a garden can be a brown bog and the next day a riot of bright yellow dandelions. They're certainly quick off the mark. That means you'd better be, too. Before you know it, every one of those flowers will be an explosion of winged seed, and quick action now can save you a lot of grief. Although dandelions are deep- and tap-rooted, they come up easily at this stage (use the long-handled, forked deep weeder described in *Tools*, page 99).

So, your soil has passed the test. At last you're out in the garden. If you didn't cut down and cart off everything last fall that's going to be your first job. There are two schools of thought about garden cleanup and the best time of year to do it. I prefer the fall, though I am sometimes prevented from doing it then by weather. A long wet autumn, ending abruptly with a hard freeze makes the job impossible. The advantages I see to end-of-season cleanup are twofold: it relieves the workload the following spring when everything needs to be done at once, and when all the dead plant material is removed you can put on clean mulch where it's needed, confident that you have lessened the risks of disease and pests.

There are gardeners (among them persuasive writers) who choose to leave everything until spring. They maintain that plants that are hard to cut in fall will be dry and brittle after the winter and snap off easily at ground level in spring. They say also that the standing plants are a mulch for the garden, and they have a point here. I see two drawbacks to this course of action, however. The young shoots of early rising perennials will be pushing up through the previous year's dead stems before the cleanup begins and might well be injured by pulling or cutting. Furthermore, some fibrous plants—Siberian iris, for instance—can be nearly impossible to cut after a long wet winter.

Ornamental grasses can, and should, stand all winter, whatever your philosophy. They are an addition to the winter landscape. Cut them down as early in spring as you can, before new growth appears.

As soon as you see the early growth of peonies and baby's breath, but before they make much top growth, put the supports in place—stakes for a stockade or wire cages (see *Supporting the Weak*, page 165).

While the soil is still relatively soft, and it will be for a while, lay down your board to stand on when you're working. It spreads the weight and you won't end up with big boot imprints. Move the board from time to time. As, year by year, your flower beds get fuller there may not be room for a board; then use two flat stones or pieces of paving.

As you go about clearing up, taking off the mulch, planting, fertilizing, and doing all the other spring tasks, keep a sharp eye out for the late risers that are likely to be damaged by the spade. Plants like balloon flower, butterfly weed, and Japanese anemone don't show for several weeks after most other plants are up. Even if you did the right thing the previous year, and marked their location, there remains the problem of "Did I put the marker in front or behind the plant, and how far out is it likely to send up shoots?" One thing is certain; once you've destroyed a favorite plant that way, your autumn labeling will ever thereafter be exemplary.

There will be many little green, as yet unidentifiable, leaves appearing almost daily at this time of year. Some of them will be welcome bonuses from good plants that seed themselves reliably, but others will be weeds. Many conscientious gardeners, forking over their borders vigorously and thoroughly, will never know how many more little perennial plants they might have gained. On the other hand, of course, they may never get to enjoy the quantity of pigweed, chickweed, sourgrass, and the like, that will be flourishing, while the overcautious gardener waits to see what's what.

Take heart: gradually, you'll be able to recognize more plants by their young leaves. At first I used to weed conscientiously under the big lavender bushes until, one day, my handful of tiny "weeds" smelt strongly of lavender, and I realized what I had pulled up. I could never mistake even the tiniest lavender seedlings now.

It's helpful to be able to recognize the seedling stage of whatever are the Top Ten weeds in your area. There are some handy back-pocket-size booklets on common weeds, with excellent drawings for identification.

Somewhere between good plants and weeds in my spring garden are the hundreds of Johnny-jump-ups (*Viola tricolor*) and forget-me-nots (*Myosotis*). These small flowers give me great pleasure. I leave some and pull up others, confident there will be enough seed for another spring. The variations in the little faces and colors of the Johnny-jump-ups are simply not to be missed.

Occasionally, there is one so lovely it becomes a player in a small exquisite scene. I remember a deep maroon and primrose yellow one. Left to grow, it was tall enough to weave into a purple annual heliotrope and a pale yellow columbine. What a picture! I haven't seen a Johnny-jump-up quite like that one since, but I must be hoping because I know that each year I let more seedlings grow tall—just in case.

If you plan to apply fertilizer, do it early in the spring. Be careful, with chemical fertilizer particularly, not to let it touch any damp young growth, as it will burn. Less harsh fertilizers include compost and aged manure.

This is the time to divide overgrown clumps of perennials. Big, heavy growers like Siberian iris, daylilies, shasta daisies, and many fall asters will be easy now, difficult later. There will be just enough growth above ground for you to see what you're doing, but not so much leaf growth as to make it hard for the plant to recover (see *Multiplication by Division*, page 78). For the same reason, this is the ideal time to move plants around in the border (see page 96). (Wouldn't last year's notebook be handy here, if only you could find it?)

You will also be putting in any stock received from mail order nurseries. Dormant, bare-root plants will have the advantage; without leaves there is little danger of loss of moisture. Leafy plants, however, have a hard struggle until they're well rooted, what with the variable spring weather and that surprisingly powerful spring sun. So be ready to shade them during the day with peach baskets. I use the baskets for a few days, removing them at night to give plants the benefit of the dew. Do not use plastic waste bins, pails, or other receptacles that will exclude air or your plants will overheat and die.

A bottomless peach basket makes a temporary cover for a tender plant.

On the subject of dividing, there's one special class of plant that will need attention early in the spring. If you have hardy chrysanthemums (*Dendranthema*) in the garden, they'll need dividing now. My method is to dig the whole plant (they're shallow-rooted) and pull off a few pieces from the outside, discarding and composting the remainder. The "offshoots" should be planted out in a nursery bed, fed and watered, and will themselves be flowering plants by fall. When they show buds, usually in late August or early September, you can move them into places in the border where you want them to bloom.

An important job just now is to cut back small shrubs you may have growing with the herbaceous perennials in the border. Some of them might more accurately be called subshrubs because they are only partly woody and often die back so far in harsh winters that they must be severely pruned or even cut to the ground. After that they behave like herbaceous perennials, responding with vigorous new growth.

In my garden, an attractive shrub, commonly called blue mist (*Caryopteris* × *clandonensis*), recovers quickly and blooms delightfully in August. Another, this time a shrubby cinquefoil, *Potentilla fruticosa*, treated the same way, covers itself with flowers almost immediately and continues to bloom off and on throughout the summer. The one I like is 'Abbotswood' because the little white flowers are so cheery and the annual shearing keeps it to a pleasantly low rounded shape.

Early in May, the shape of beds and borders is clearly visible.

Mid-July, and the garden is at its peak in color, form, and texture.

The garden in June, with grass at its greenest, and yellow, white, and blue as the principal flower colors

By mid-August, the colors have heated up. Rich reds and golden yellows catch the morning sun.

Lupins have a substantial quality that is particularly valuable in the spring garden. The blue iris is Iris sibirica 'Super Ego'.

The Siberian iris 'White Swirl' is a standout in the garden for two weeks in late June. It is a perfect accompaniment in color and form to the foxgloves, the tall blue anchusa, and a pink oriental poppy.

With fewer flowers in bloom, form is more easily perceived. In the near bed, the beauty of the broad leaves of Hosta 'Gold Standard' is enhanced by the swordlike leaves of an early Siberian iris, 'Little White'. Across the path, the later, tall Siberian iris 'White Swirl' is in full bloom.

Sedum 'Autumn Joy' (foreground), showing green flowers in early August, will be copper-red by September. The lavender spires of Russian sage (Perovskia atriplicifolia) show to advantage against the purple leaves of Perilla frutescens. The bright phlox is 'Sandra'.

Ligularia 'The Rocket' dominates the yellow side of the long border. Daylilies and the yarrow 'Coronation Gold' are sturdy mid-border plants. 'Moonbeam', the pale-yellow threadleaf coreopsis in the foreground, blooms all summer. A tall Canadian burnet, Sanguisorba canadensis, is just opening its white bottlebrush flowers. More white is provided by Artemisia lactiflora and a white balloon flower.

Across the garden in early August. The deep-red dahlia in the foreground is 'Arabian Nights'.

In a border backed by ferns, a froth of false baby's breath (Galium aristata) hides the leggy stems of the tall rose 'Queen Elizabeth'.

Stone walls at either end of the long border contain it and give it solidity. Sedum 'Autumn Joy' is substantial enough to hold its own visually against the flat stones of the near wall.

The pastel side of the long border is highlighted by a purple balloon flower and a pink coneflower. The rose-red phlox 'Leo Schlageter' puts a little bite into the color scheme.

Phlox is the mainstay of the red bed in July and August. The bold cherry-red 'Sandra' is a strong bloomer. Behind it, a crimson bee balm, 'Colrain Red', grows like a hedge. Russian sage and annual heliotrope in the foreground offer tint and shade of the same color.

Swamp maple, birch, and poplar along the driveway rival the garden in color in October.

With the annuals killed by frost, a few perennials tough it out. The big sedum 'Autumn Joy' fulfills its promise, and the aster 'Purple Dome' lives up to its name.

Japanese painted fern is delightful in a ground cover of starry phlox.

An unlikely, yet pleasing, color combination: the oriental poppy 'Beauty of Livermore' and a tall bearded iris, 'Heavenly Blue'.

My "meadow" garden. Yellow and orange hawkweed take over a poor stretch of ground.

Perfect for the wedding month—roses and lilies in June

Blue oat grass, Helictotrichon sempervirens, *in its early summer bloom*

The Hidcote strain of lavender is the darkest purple. The lavender's woody branches help to contain exuberant poppies.

The annual
satinflower (Godetia)
in crimson, pink, and
white appeals to
everyone who sees
it. Why isn't it grown
more often?

The color and form of knotweed (Polygonum bistortum), Siberian iris 'Fairy Dawn', and purple clustered bellflower (Campanula glomerata) fill a corner in spring.

An unusual pairing of colors: a rose-pink gas plant with columbines in lemon and coral

*White meadowsweet (Filipendula hexapetala)
and pink meadowrue (Thalictrum
aquilegifolium) lend dignity and height to the
late spring border. A small iris, Iris pallida
'Variegata', shows off its lilac flowers in the
front of the border.*

*With so many different plants in a small
section of the garden, color is an important
consideration. The white offered by the
peach-leaved bellflower and the phlox 'Miss
Lingard' and the cream of the small perennial
foxglove enliven the mauve and purple of the
plants in the foreground.*

A low stone wall is a good place to grow some of the small sedums.

The lightest breeze and the airy branches of Crambe cordifolia make an Impressionist picture with the flat golden disks of fernleaf yarrow 'Coronation Gold'.

An empty space beside a stone path calls for a mature plant—in this case, a well-grown Coral Bells (Heuchera sanguinea).

Digging a good-sized hole gives any plant a good start in life.

A strong jet of water from the hose will settle the soil down around the roots.

Other shrubs with considerable winter dieback that benefit from hard pruning in early spring are the purple-leaved smokebush (*Cotinus coggygria*) and the oak-leaf hydrangea (*Hydrangea quercifolia*).

Two more plants need your attention at this time of year. Russian sage (*Perovskia atriplicifolia*), generally listed as a herbaceous perennial but occasionally as a subshrub, must be pruned back to stubs of a few inches, or cut totally to the ground, to encourage fresh growth and generous bloom. I have to admit here to cowardly behavior—always pruning to stubs and never quite cutting all the way to the ground, because I'm so afraid it's not going to bloom in time. *Perovskia* needs a hot dry summer and should be grown in full sun to be at its best.

Lavender, the second plant, is a whole study in itself. I grow *Lavandula angustifolia* in the Hidcote strain. This is the dark purple variety, and relatively slow growth is the price you pay for this rich color. Its performance—for lavender growing in a Zone 5 garden—is good, on the whole, but there are losses some years and the plants never attain the size of the lavenders seen in England. It wouldn't be a garden for me without them, however, and I enjoy giving them the attention they need in spring. Most years, I leave the flower stalks on at the end of summer—no point in pruning twice a year. I do the annual shearing in late spring, often as late as the first week in June (lavender blooms on new growth, so there's no danger of losing flowers). With a pair of two-handled grass shears, I go over each bush, shearing to a rounded shape. I can make the cut as high or low as I wish; in a matter of one or two weeks, tiny green buds show at the cut, and purple buds appear on the new growth in another two or three weeks. Every year it's a miracle. (Don't be in a hurry to declare lavender dead; it stays gray for a long time. See *Cuttings*, page 82).

Lavender bushes are a sorry sight in spring but respond well to a hard shearing. Watch for the little buds that appear magically, even on what appears to be hard, gray wood.

There are other spring pruning jobs that can be left a little longer. In cold climates, modern roses are "iffy" at best, and they call for a period of watchful waiting. The only modern rose I grow is 'Queen Elizabeth' (*Rosa grandiflora*) and I'm here to sing its praises. Few plants could look deader in April or even early May—I know I dug up good roses years ago, assuming they were dead—but few plants can get their act together more rapidly. I hold off pruning until I see signs of life. By late June this remarkable rose will present the first of the three flushes of bloom. The last one lights up the border in October.

Some shrubs don't need early pruning. Spring-bloomers such as forsythia, lilac, and others that set flower buds a year ahead are pruned only after they have bloomed. (Aren't you glad there's one job, at least, that can wait a little while?)

If you're growing your own annuals from seed, you'll have to keep a watchful eye on them too, while you're doing all these other things. Most of them will have to be hardened off gradually, and will not go into the garden until after the last frost date (see *Seeding*, page 68). I find I can make an exception of snapdragons. They prefer cool weather and will take off and make strong bushy plants, ready to bloom in June.

Although I don't use a lot of fertilizer, preferring to get some good compost in under everything I plant, I do like to add soluble fertilizer when watering annuals after transplanting. Follow the instructions, using the solution at half the strength recommended on the package (see *How I Plant*, page 88).

Is it still spring? If we don't hurry it will be summer before we get to moving the biennials, taking cuttings, seeding annuals in odd spaces . . . but isn't that just exactly what happens in gardens? Just for a moment, imagine some of the many things that could put you completely out of the running for any garden work in these important months of the year: you win a trip around the world; your job requires you to be on the other side of the country for two months; unexpectedly, you fall in love—with a determined nongardener. Any number of things can happen to take you away from your garden.

So the next time you look at your garden it's July. What will you see? Certainly it won't be neat. There will be a mass of flowers and weeds that might even look beautiful from a distance; if you had a lawn it will now be hopeless, and you had better call someone at once. Paths will be weedy and overrun by plants at the front of the border. Everything will be tall. There will be seed heads on plants that bloomed while there was nobody there to deadhead them, and you may be surprised at their beauty. The weak will have been taken over by the strong. The flowers of late summer, always among the stalwart, are getting ready to bloom.

In fact, your garden will have survived. A flower garden can take a year of this kind of neglect and still be brought back (two years, though, would be too much). So what if you didn't move the biennials, you didn't take cuttings, you didn't divide the big perennials? Relax and enjoy your jungle for now. Do a mammoth cleanup in autumn and take comfort in the thought that there's always next year.

Set out on cold white paper like this, the number of things that have to be done—apparently on that one good day in spring—look overwhelming. You might stop and ask yourself how many gardeners will have checked off all the spring jobs on their list. Very few, I suspect. Yet the gardens look all right. The gardeners are the only ones who know what they didn't quite get to. Remember, this thing of gardening is something we're doing because we love it and because we want to do it. What a pity if we went grubbing along, heads down, shortsightedly jabbing at weeds, and never taking a moment to straighten up and see the beauty all around us.

Once every year, and it's always in May, I tell classes and lecture audiences, and anyone who'll listen, to reflect with the poet W. H. Davies:

> "What is this life if, full of care,
> We have no time to stand and stare?"

CHAPTER 5

. . . .

FILLING THE BEDS AND BORDERS

*T*he space you've prepared for your flower garden probably looks enormous—enormous and bare—and all you want to do is fill it with plants as quickly as possible. So what are your options?

You have several. You can shop for container-grown plants at local nurseries and garden centers. You can order plants either bare-root or potted from mail-order nurseries. Growing from seed is another, inexpensive way to fill a bed. Big field-grown clumps, freshly dug by local growers, are a good bet when you can find them. Finally, those "pass-along" plants from friends can fill a lot of holes.

WHAT'S IN A NAME?

When I was just beginning a perennial garden I decided I needed good, tough performers that would make a bold show in the big space I had. Perennial cornflowers would be just right, I thought, so I ordered some. They arrived looking just fine, and I planted them where their spiky, reddish purple flowers would give bold color early in the year.

Everything grew up fast. There were no cornflowers that I could see, but I did notice some awkward-looking yellow mopheads, like huge thistles. To the books, then, only to find that the single entry, cornflower, led me to eleven different plants, all beginning with *Centaurea*. I skimmed through the pictures and found that the one I wanted was *Centaurea montana*, whereas the one I had was *C. macrocephala* (and sure enough it was "large-headed") and they were about as different from each other as two plants could be. Lesson learned. I realized that to get what I wanted I would have to ask for it by its correct name.

It's not snobbery, and people are not necessarily showing off when they give a plant its full name; they are according it a specific identity. This is practical, and can save you the waste of a whole garden season of growing the wrong thing.

I shall not do more here than tell you, in a sentence, that the present binomial system of naming plants was worked out over two hundred years ago by the Swedish botanist Linnaeus. At this point you might like to know that the rules are established, enforced—and, for all I know, even bent sometimes—by two august bodies: the International Code of Botanical Nomenclature and the International Code of Nomenclature for Cultivated Plants.

When I tell you that *Dianthus caryophyllus* is the correct name for a clove pink, you might think it a bit cumbersome, but you should have been around before Linnaeus. The late A. W. Smith, that learned and helpful plant-name specialist, tells us that clove pink was then *Dianthus floribus solitaris, squamis calycinic subovatis brevissimis, corollis crenatis.* (His translation: Dianthus with solitary flowers, with very short inverted egg-shaped, scaled calyces and crown-shaped corollas!)

Each plant name, in italics, begins with the genus, with an initial capital letter. It is followed by the species, with a lower-case initial letter. In many instances, a cultivar name may follow, capitalized and between single quotation marks, but not italicized.

So let's take a lovely border phlox, *Phlox paniculata* 'Starfire,' as an example. The first word covers the whole genus; the second is the species, and is very important (there are at least ten common species of phlox, ranging from a prostrate ground cover to a stately plant of two- to four feet). In this case, *paniculata* tells you that the flower heads are arranged in panicles, or spreading clusters. The third word is the cultivar. 'Starfire' is a clear, brilliant red; 'Bright Eyes' is a twinkly pink-and-red; 'Dresden China' is a soft, pearly pink; 'World Peace' is a large, late white; and so on.

Emphasizing correct nomenclature is not to suggest that we throw out all the common names of plants. Many are charming and evocative, and it would be a pity if they were lost. I like some of them so much that they come into my head every time I look at the plant. There is a modest little plant beside a grass path in my garden, a typical cottage garden plant, called *Astrantia major*. A collar of stiff white bracts, flushed pink and green, surround each tiny, packed flowerhead.

It's easy to see how it came by the name of Hattie's Pincushion, but I'm puzzled by its other name, Melancholy Gentleman.

I grow a gaudy dianthus for its unsophisticated but affectionately bestowed name of Dad's Favorite. One almost sees Dad trimming its blue-green foliage and snipping a flower for his buttonhole. And what about Gardener's Garters, Creeping Jenny, Dusky Cranesbill, and Devil's Paintbrush, known in Elizabethan England as Grim, the Collier?

Folksy names, while charming, are very little use when you're ordering plants. To me, bluebells are the bulbs that carpet English beech woods in spring (*Scilla nonscripta*), but there are the bluebells of Scotland (*Campanula rotundiflora*), and, most familiar to American gardeners, Virginia bluebells (*Mertensia virginica*). I have seen grape hyacinths (*Muscari botryoides*) and even Jacob's ladder (*Polemonium caeruleum*) offered as bluebells.

Enough said?

*P*ASS-ALONGS

To take the last of these first, friends and neighbors may well press plants upon you, and at first you'll probably take them all. I think the principal feeling of new or beginning gardeners is gratitude, gratitude for almost everything you're given—even though you may have to spend the next few years digging it out (I actually thanked someone once for a clump of mint and witchgrass!). It stands to reason that plants so freely given away are likely to be rampant spreaders. But there you are with all that space, so this may not be the time to be choosy.

Do be aware, however, that some gifts are going to be better than others. It's safe to take whatever you're offered in the way of daylilies and Siberian iris—they're great multipliers and space fillers yet easily moved and divided later. Keep an eagle eye however, on the bully plants. Some of them, like gooseneck loosestrife and bishop's weed, are out to take over the world. Before long, when you're a knowledgeable and choosy gardener yourself, you'll be able to pass extra plants to other starting gardeners who will be very glad to have them, just as you were.

*F*IELD-DUG PLANTS

Well, that's it for freebies. But you can add to those big plants that you've been given by buying freshly dug field-grown plants. Such plants will do a lot to help fill up a garden. If you watch your local newspaper you'll often see these advertised by enterprising amateurs. I head over with my peach baskets or cardboard cartons. There I see what I want and have them dug for me. Such plants are not expensive and they'll be strong and good-sized, so they'll give you a good effect without waiting a year or more.

Another advantage to field-dug plants is that they won't have to be out of the ground a long time. You bring them right home in your car and put them into the prepared bed. The plants will be fine as long as you water them and perhaps shade them for a day, if they need it. They'll grow right along and sometimes will hardly know that they've been moved.

*B*UYING LOCALLY

For a new gardener I recommend buying container-grown plants from a local nursery or garden center. You can often see the plant in bloom so you'll know whether it's what you want or not. And if you scout out all possible local sources— and I'm happy to say that they are growing in number all the time—you'll discover which have the superior plants.

A container-grown plant like this one from a local nursery will make a smooth transition from pot to flower bed.

There is an added advantage—when you go to buy your plants you can usually find some knowledgeable person to talk to. The decision whether to buy the smaller or larger plants will be governed by your pocketbook. If you've gathered information about these plants you'll have some idea of their rate of growth. If it's a fast-growing plant you'll do quite well to buy a small one. If it's slow-growing, why wait two years? You want results as quickly as possible.

*B*UYING BY MAIL

We'll assume that for months you've been reading about plants. You may have subscribed to a magazine or two; you're probably looking in the newspapers for garden columns and seasonal articles. Perhaps you've watched other gardeners and you have an idea that there are some plants that you would like and that you don't see at your local nursery. You will have to send for catalogs. Now comes pure joy; you can indulge yourself in daydreams. The hardest thing will be saying no and cutting down your list. (This is easier to do when you add up the numbers in the right-hand column. I find this cuts the list down pretty quickly.)

There are advantages and disadvantages to ordering by mail. You may be able to get some uncommon plants, but a drawback will be that they'll have to be in transit for several days unless you want to pay extra for express delivery. Many will be quite small; obviously, a large plant in a big pot of soil will arrive with a considerable added shipping cost.

More important than these disadvantages is one you may not have thought of. Some of these uncommon plants you want are being grown and sold by nurseries several zones warmer than yours. No wonder you haven't seen them in gardens on your neighborhood walks! So take care to order plants that will survive in your climate.

Mail-order nurseries offer plants either bare-root or potted in a growing medium. Bare-root plants, mostly trees and shrubs but some perennials, too, have usually been dug in the fall and held over in cold storage all winter. They don't begin to grow until you plant them. They look very dispiriting when you take them out of the package, but most, roses in particular, do very well when they're shipped in this way. (Once my husband, unwrapping two young apple trees, was heard to say with some indignation, "Someone has sent you two sticks.")

When the plants arrive potted in a growing medium, you'll discover that the packing from some nurseries holds up better than that from others. For this reason, among others, you should unwrap any package as soon as it arrives. Some nurseries offer packs of three or six of the same kind, individually potted. Generally, the plants will be young and small and probably won't bloom the first year, but they are much less expensive. Plant them out in well-prepared soil to be sure they make good root growth, and they'll be beautiful in the second year. Of course they are less expensive—you're doing part of the work of bringing them on; the price goes up when the nursery has to hold them for another whole year.

If you can't plant them the minute they arrive, water the plants and put them in a shaded, protected place for a couple of days. They've been in a box, remember, for at least three or four days before you get them.

These little mail-order plants have been recovering in a shady spot for several days. Planted in compost-rich soil, they will make good growth in only two or three weeks.

"FEATURE" PLANTS

Make a determined effort as soon as possible to get in a few of the strong "place holders" or "feature" plants that will help you keep your bearings as you are planting the border. I'm thinking of such plants as peonies, bearded iris, and oriental poppies.

The standard recommendation is to plant these as dormant roots, which means late summer for the poppies and bearded iris, and fall for peonies. They are carried by most mail-order houses, but are the specialty of a few. Plants must be ordered well before planting time to ensure getting the cultivars you want.

Since the advent of the "instant" container-grown plant at local nurseries, all three have been available in one- or two-gallon pots, and I know several gardeners who have been pleased with plants bought this way. For myself, I have shied away from buying the growing peony plants because when last I looked they were offered only under "white, pink, red," and I was looking for named cultivars. I see that these, too, are now offered container-grown, so my objection is no longer valid. Nevertheless, I would rather plant a dormant root and give it the opportunity to spread out where it wants than buy a potted plant that might be strangling in its own roots.

What does a gardener do for the first year, having missed the boat on the ordering? That might be the moment for container-grown plants, but I would still recommend sending for the specialty catalogs in addition, and getting an order in for the next season.

Don't be shocked when your package arrives. Dormant is hardly the word. The oriental poppy may have a few little crinkled leaves around it, but the peony is a very weird sight, and the iris rhizomes resemble failed potatoes (see *Plants with Special Requirements*, page 97.)

These plants go into the ground right away, and you probably won't see anything of them until the next spring. They take a long time to get established, to grow big and solid-looking, but they are going to last for years and are going to help give your garden a feeling of permanence. Should you need a sobering thought, remember that peonies often outlive the gardeners who plant them.

GROWING FROM SEED

I expect you're waiting for the end of this list of ways to get plants for your border, and wondering when you're going to come to seeding. It sounds like an inexpensive way to increase your plant stock. It is not, however, inexpensive in time and labor, and you may want to leave this particular operation for later, when your garden is further along.

Having said that, I still hope you'll try it, because it's an exciting, even miraculous, process. In general, annuals are easily grown from seed. They are a good bet if you are planning to make your first foray into seeding and if, as is likely, you have large spaces to fill the first year.

Perennials are another matter. Some of the kind you're likely to want—phlox and oriental poppies, for instance—cannot be relied on to come true to type, although occasionally seeding will give you variations in color and form that you might find more attractive than the original.

Annuals

I shall always buy most of my annuals from a local nursery. They are healthy, uniform plants, they're earlier than anything I can raise indoors with my various improvisations, and they certainly save me an enormous amount of trouble. And yet . . . and yet . . . Every year, I order seeds of a few favorite annuals and grow them myself, some directly in the borders and others in rows in the production garden, to be moved to the border in late summer.

I do this because there is an easy, bountiful look about a direct-sown mass of such annuals as candytuft, baby's breath, tobacco flowers, or other such informal plants. This look is harder to achieve when you're setting out plants you've bought by the half dozen. No matter how hard you try, you find yourself putting them in rows or blocks and they have a regimented look. Direct seeding avoids that awkward effect.

I sometimes hedge my bets, putting out a half-dozen nursery-raised plants and scattering seed of the same species among them. This results in an attractive mass of flowers with staggered blooming times.

Be sure to check the information on the seed packet. Is this a frost-hardy annual that can be sown as soon as the soil is workable in spring? If not, and it is a tender annual, then it should not be sown until after the latest frost date in your area, in which case you might consider sowing earlier indoors, to get a jump on the season.

SOWING ANNUAL SEEDS IN THE BORDER

Here's what I do when I sow annuals directly into the border:

- Clear the area of stones and cultivate until the soil has a fine, crumbly texture.
- Outline the shape to be planted, using a thin sprinkling of lime or fertilizer.
- Water the prepared soil thoroughly.
- Put a thin layer of vermiculite or other seed-starting medium on top of the moist soil.
- Sprinkle seeds thinly on the surface. Some flower seeds need light to germinate and should be pressed down lightly but not covered. Some require a light covering, and a few germinate better in the dark and will take a cover of planting mix about a quarter of an inch deep. Follow the instructions on the package to determine the depth at which each variety should be planted. Remember, though, that the most common cause of failure with seeds is planting too deeply.
- Firm the whole surface gently.

Resist the urge to water at this stage; you might wash all the seeds into one clump. Furthermore, it is not needed; the moisture from the watered garden soil will have spread to the seed layer when you pressed it down.

Conditions in early spring, when the garden is still holding winter moisture, are generally favorable to seeding but watering will be important from now until germination to prevent the surface of the seedbed from drying out.

To the gardener, this is a seedbed. Cats perceive it otherwise. You might as well hang out a sign: "Kitty Comfort Station." To deal with this problem, I lay crumpled chicken wire—light enough not to suppress the emerging seedlings— over the seedbed, and it evidently reduces the comfort sufficiently to keep cats off.

If, despite your careful sowing, the seedlings are unevenly distributed and too crowded in places, thin them out a little. I find it does less damage if I use scissors and cut off the unwanted seedlings at the soil line, rather than pulling them out in clumps.

At the same time that I'm seeding in the borders, I seed a few annuals in rows in the production garden. These are for moving into the border later in the summer, when their color and form are needed, so they have to be easy to transplant. Cosmos, nicotiana, and snapdragons are excellent for this purpose.

The recommended procedure for sowing in rows calls for using a hoe, but I find this makes too deep a furrow. I lay a long broomstick on the ground and press it down just enough to make a shallow trough. I'm a bit more fussy when I sow seeds in rows than when I scatter them in the border. I'm extra careful to sow thinly, and am more disciplined at thinning them out so that when the time comes to transplant they can be lifted singly without disturbing a whole clump of plants.

The care and feeding of annual seedlings is the same wherever they're grown. Soluble fertilizer at half the strength recommended on the package is helpful every time you water while the plants are making rapid growth, and after that they will do well on their own. Annuals are not heavy feeders and, in any case, heavy fertilizing will give you too much leaf and scant bloom.

Perennials

In spite of everything said about the drawbacks to raising perennials from seed, there are a few I enjoy growing this way. Most perennials should be sown soon after blooming time if you want them to reach a safe size before winter. Even then, I leave them in the rows until the following spring, because that first winter can be very hard on young plants that have not had time to develop a strong root system.

Certain perennial seeds require what is known as "stratification," a period of chilling, before they will germinate. This can complicate things in the average garden because the seeds may just sit there in their rows all winter and not appear until the following spring. A few—primroses, for instance—are so persnickety that they can sit out *two* winters before making an appearance. What do you bet you'll have dug them up or planted something on top of them by then? I've had a few interesting duplex plantings myself, but I can't recommend it. Some perennials, like columbine and echinacea, in my garden, for example, self-sow freely and I enjoy the many colors I get from this open pollination.

In addition, I buy new seed of some perennials for indoor growing. Sown early in spring, they bloom six months later. This is not the usual timetable for perennials, which don't bloom until their second year, but it has a special advantage. Delphinium, for example, seeded indoors in February, are set out in the garden in early June and make excellent growth. In late August and September, they bloom (albeit on short stems), giving me a chance to choose the colors I want for transplanting into the borders. The following year, they're back on schedule and blooming in June with their elegant spires on regular-sized plants.

I know I could—and often do—seed these plants in rows out in the garden. My indoor seeding is a sometime thing. I do it in years when I have both the time and the inclination. I take the greatest pleasure in looking at the little seed boxes under lights in the basement. Small miracles, these—plants not yet an inch high, yet perfect miniatures of their full-grown selves.

Biennials

Biennials are so valuable in the early summer garden that it's worth reminding yourself to grow them every year. I seed foxgloves, Canterbury bells, and sweet William outside, as early in the summer as possible. They are usually good-sized plants by early September and I like to move them into the places where I want them to bloom the following May. All three grow from leafy rosettes, providing their own mulch for winter.

I remember well a winter with no snow for protection, and the weather fluctuating wildly between icy and warm. There were dreadful losses among all plants, but some caused more distress than others. It wasn't until we had a spring without the lovely spires of foxglove and the glowing bells of campanula that I fully realized their worth in the garden.

FILLING IN THE GAPS

Now take a look at your flower bed. You have all these plants—from friends, from mail-order companies, from local nurseries, field-dug plants, and the promise

The garden that looked so empty in early May can put on a generous show by July.

of peonies and oriental poppies to come—yet there's still a lot of empty space because you had to allow these plants room to grow. They're going to take a lot more space as they get bigger, but you want something to get you through that first year.

This is where annuals come in. I had to start with annuals the first year at

Heath because, having begun my garden in May, that was the only way I was going to have any color that season. Annuals can serve you well in the short term, while you're building up your long-term perennial plantings.

A word here about the smart way to buy annuals. You don't need them big and blooming because you know what they're going to look like. Every book, every catalog has pictures of them in flower, and the nursery packs will be labeled. You want them when they're small, green, and bushy; they take transplanting better and will make stronger plants.

Keep a close eye on that bed in its first summer, and, at season's end, take stock. It looks pretty full—very little bare earth to be seen. But wait . . . How many of those plants are annuals? Annuals that will be gone after frost? Unless you want to buy and plant a lot of annuals each spring, perhaps you need more perennials. Now, let's look at the ways you can get more plants from the ones you have.

The small plants on the left are the best buy. The leggy ones on the right may have blossoms but will not make attractive, bushy plants unless you cut them back before planting.

GOOD OLD RELIABLES: A BAKER'S DOZEN

This was to have been called "Foolproof Perennials," until I realized it sounded insulting both to the planters and the planted. But believe me when I tell you that these perennials really are the most accommodating and reliable of plants, as close to indestructible as living things are likely to be.

There are no prima donnas here, nor shy, retiring violets. All are plants of sufficient size to make a show in a beginning garden. They have had to satisfy a number of requirements for inclusion in this list. They should be:

- Hardy through Zone 5 without special protection;
- Good growers, meaning that they take off fast when planted; increase generously without being invasive, and divide easily;
- Resistant to disease and insect pests without the gardener's having to resort to sprays;
- Once established, able to get along without much watering;
- Strong enough to stand up without elaborate and expensive devices;
- In bloom over a long period or capable of two flushes of bloom in the season.

They get extra points if they make good cutting flowers and are not unduly reckless with their seed.

So, here are the paragons—a baker's dozen of them. Well, one or two almost flunked. Michaelmas daisies can have a problem with mildew (though not every year); so can phlox; four others are somewhat overgenerous with their seed. You may notice that eight out of the total are daisylike in flower. They are listed here in order of blooming time.

EARLY SUMMER

Perennial cornflower, mountain bluet (Centaurea montana)

A strong color note in the early border. 1 to 1½ feet high. Reddish purple flower heads like big versions of the annual bachelor's button. A vigorous grower—you will be able to divide it by the second year. Generous with its seeds. Cut it down when the leaves begin to yellow—it will make new leaves and flowers.

Golden marguerite, false chamomile *(Anthemis tinctoria)*

I call this the ultimate daisy. Hundreds of daisies, most often bright yellow, though some cultivars in a softer hue. Ferny foliage. 2 to 3 feet high. Seeds as if there were no tomorrow. Good cutting flower.

Siberian iris *(Iris sibirica)*

A wonder plant. (Not to be confused with bearded iris, which are much more work.) The narrow, swordlike foliage is elegant throughout the season. Height from 2 feet ('Caesar's Brother' dark purple) to 3 feet ('White Swirl'). There is also an engaging 'Little White,' not much more than 12 inches high. Rainbow colors. Clumps grow very big, at which stage dividing them is a two-gardener job (see page 79).

Peach-leaved bellflower *(Campanula persicifolia)*

A graceful little bell tower, 2 feet tall, in white or blue, rising from a rosette of narrow leaves. The only drawback to this plant is the tedium of deadheading, flower by flower, if you want to keep it blooming. You will want to, once you have seen the early morning light caught in those delicate bells.

MIDSUMMER AND ON

Bee balm, Oswego tea *(Monarda didyma)*

You have to plant this for the hummingbirds, but it will do you good, too, with its rich color and minty aroma. At 2 to 3 feet, on strong square stems, it flowers in scarlet, pink, crimson, and purple (also white, but who would want it—certainly not the hummingbirds in my garden, who choose the red). Often described as "invasive," but don't be afraid; you can pull up the shallow-rooted mat very easily.

Tickseed *(Coreopsis grandiflora; C. lanceolata)*

Another archetypal daisy, 1 to 2 feet high, long-blooming, in neon yellow. For a gentler effect, try threadleaf coreopsis (*C. verticillata*), smaller, with needlelike foliage. One cultivar, 'Moonbeam', is *de rigueur* in gardens today—not just trendy, however, but lovely in palest yellow.

Shasta daisy *(Chrysanthemum × superbum)*

Cultivars range in height from 12-inch 'Little Miss Muffet' (not for me—I dislike standard-size flowers on dwarf plants) to 2-foot 'Alaska', one of the hardiest, as you might gather from its name. Great performers. Keep deadheading, then cutting back, and you'll have these big white daisies most of the summer.

Garden phlox *(Phlox paniculata)*

Now here's a flower with no common name (*Phlox*, from the Greek, means "flame") but that doesn't seem to faze people. If they can manage Greek, I wonder, why can't they manage Latin names? Height usually 2 to 3 feet, but a few go to 4 feet in my garden. Yes, it can get mildewed, in which case you cut it down and let it start again. But don't let that keep this lovely thing—the very essence of summer—out of your garden. I grow fourteen different colors—everything but yellow and true blue (see list on page 152). For beauty in September and October, try tall, white 'World Peace', the last phlox of the year.

Purple coneflower *(Echinacea purpurea)*

A true American native, often described as "coarse," though I think it romantic, probably from reading Willa Cather's novels about the prairies. Grow it for strength; rigid rough stems go to 3 or 4 feet and bear large daisy flowers with reflexed petals. 'Bright Star' is rose pink; 'White Lustre' is an old ivory white, on a shorter plant. It certainly does seed, resulting in a variety of shades of pink, but I like to see birds on the seed heads in fall, so I always leave a few standing.

Daylily *(Hemerocallis)*

What can I add to all that has been written about this answer to a gardener's prayer? Its range extends over seven zones. It fires up hybridizers—professional and amateur alike—to produce hundreds of new ones every year (resulting in some bizarre cultivar names). The lemon lily (*H. lilioasphodelus*) spreads its delicious fragrance early in the season. The daylily of roadsides, the tawny daylily (*H. fulva*) marks the cellar holes and dooryards of houses long since gone. Send for a catalog and pick your colors.

Black-eyed Susan *(Rudbeckia fulgida)*

Another daisy. Even if you haven't heard of any other Susans, you're sure to know 'Goldsturm'. Bright yellow petals surround a brown center. Beginning in July, this plant goes on blooming up to frost. It seeds, but the resulting brood are not of the same quality; extreme popularity has resulted in some sloppy propagation.

*L*ATE SUMMER INTO FALL

Michaelmas daisy, New England aster *(Aster novae-angliae)*

From 12-inch dwarfs to giants of 6 to 7 feet. These asters are fall-blooming, and not the annual China aster (*Callistephus chinensis*). Small daisy flowers in white, pink, purple, lavender, and red. 'Alma Potschke' (2 to 3 feet) is a magnificent cultivar, with glowing rose red flowers. It blooms in my garden from early August into October and, in ten years, has shown no sign of mildew.

Sneezeweed, Helen's flower *(Helenium autumnale)*

Once again, daisylike flowers, this time on tall bushy plants 4 to 6 feet tall. Many cultivars in colors ranging from yellow to red and bronze, and the performance is spectacular. If you don't want them this tall, cut them back by a third (or more) in early summer. This one is reliable, indestructible, and—foolproof.

CHAPTER 6

. . . .

MORE PLANTS FROM WHAT YOU HAVE

C hances are good that once you've enjoyed a season or two of your new flower garden you're going to want more of everything. Where there was one plant, you now think you'd like to see a drift of two or three, or even five.

Looking at the garden in spring, you notice a good many empty spaces that last year were filled with annuals. The annuals were fine as a temporary measure, but you want to be moving toward a more perennial planting. Not only that, but over the winter you've most likely succumbed to gardeners' daydreams and are filled with visions of more and bigger flower beds.

Cheer up. Where your pocketbook might have limited your initial planting you now have the possibility of making more plants from the ones you already have, right in your own garden. Now for some ways of doing it.

*M*ULTIPLICATION BY DIVISION

The simplest and most obvious way is the plain division of the whole plant into parts. In the Northeast, this is best done in early spring, just as soon as the perennials begin to show signs of life. Bright green, curled leaf buds will show on top of the newly thawed soil, and that's a perfect time to start your propagation.

Good plants for simple division include such strong growers as phlox, asters, and helenium, to name a few of the "workhorses" of the border. Dig up the whole clump and you may see where a logical division can be made. Sometimes a plant will obligingly fall in half or in several pieces, but if it doesn't you can pull it apart with your fingers or break it up with a hand fork. You then replant the divisions just as you would with purchased plants (see *How I Plant*, page 88).

This will work well with plants that have been in place only two or three years, but in another year or two a fast-growing plant will be big enough to make the task somewhat daunting. Then you use a different technique. Dig up the plant, drive two spading forks back-to-back into the center of the plant, then lever them outward until it comes in half. With a really big clump, you can divide each in half again. The hardest part of the operation can be getting the forks out of the divisions, and I usually look for help with this.

Of course, it's possible to divide plants by driving a sharp-edged spade right down through the middle, but I have some objections to this. First, it cuts such a straight line down the center that a lot of good shoots are destroyed and, second, the divisions, to my mind, don't look rounded and natural. I've known plants divided this way to keep that unattractive straight edge for a whole season.

Two forks make the division of a large perennial a lot easier—
a good technique for border phlox, Siberian iris, and shasta daisies.

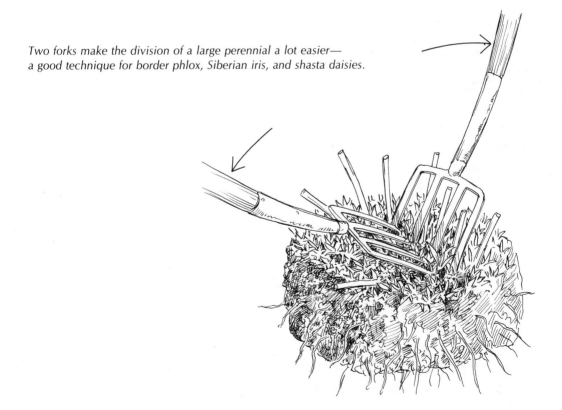

There are occasions when I adopt an entirely different procedure. Let's say there is one special plant that I need to divide but am nervous of losing. I take out "insurance." In spring, I go in under the surface of the soil and "tweak" off an outside shoot, using my fingers as they're more sensitive and discriminating than any hand tool. (Students seeing me do this invariably react with indignation: "Sure, you can do it with *your* wonderful soil, you should just see mine." Well, you should have seen *this* soil when I began [see *Gardening from the Ground Up*, page 41].) I plant that little outside shoot. If it thrives, great; if it dies, I still have the mother plant and I can try again. I've done this often with my own seed-raised delphiniums when I can't be sure of getting a particular lovely color again.

Getting more of what you have is not the only reason to divide plants. Most perennials require division periodically if they are to perform well. The Siberian iris is a good example from my own experience: I can remember some epic struggles when I left mine too long without dividing them. A healthy, vigorous plant will keep growing outward as its roots seek more food. The plant gets bigger, but you will notice that the center bears significantly fewer flowers and eventually becomes nonviable, woody tissue. This is a clear call for division, and of a more extreme kind than that described above.

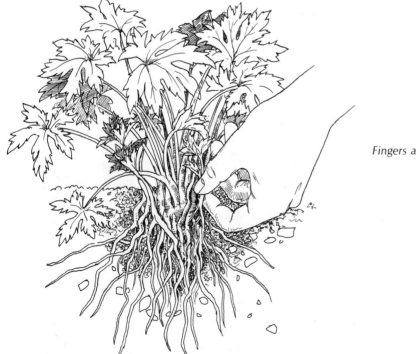

Fingers are best for "tweaking."

Two skeptical workshop students were surprised at the weight of this Siberian iris clump. With a tarpaulin, a gardener working alone could slide it from one part of the garden to another.

Dig up the whole plant (you'll be astonished at the size and weight of a mature Siberian iris). Put it on a ground sheet and haul it away to some part of the garden where you can work on it without doing damage to neighboring plants in the border. Take a sharp-edged spade and cut the whole plant mass into wedges, as if it were a pie.

This is no ordinary pie, however—the best part of each wedge is the outside crust. Cut off the pointed centers and take them to the compost pile. Thrift is all very well but this woody center has no future. Now plant out the divisions in the ordinary way (see *How I Plant*, page 88).

I add two warnings, both based on painful personal experience. First, if the plant is old and big, don't begin by whacking it in the center with the spade; you can put an elbow or shoulder out for the rest of the season. Work in from the outside edges with the sharp corner of your spade.

Second, don't fall into the trap of thinking you must plant every single piece. This procedure can give you anything from four divisions to sixteen and up, depending on the size of the original plant. Set out as many as you want, give away as many as you can, and compost the rest.

CUTTINGS

It's heady stuff, this getting something for nothing! Once you have been successful with the division technique, you'll want to try some other ways of increasing your stock of plants. Growing plants from stem and root cuttings is a tried and true method and works with many perennials. I haven't bothered to do it with plants that divide easily, but I find it a good way of getting enough chrysanthemum plants. The stem cuttings I make in early spring give me modest-sized but pleasingly shaped plants, and all of them bloom that same year.

Lavender is something of a religion with me, and I suppose always will be. I need enough plants to use as an edging to the borders. There are some losses among the older plants almost every winter, so I must have some replacements at the ready. I have found seeding to be slow and uncertain, especially in the 'Hidcote' strain, which I prefer because of its strong purple color.

So I take stem cuttings, but they are not actually *cut*. I don't use a knife. I break off shoots with a sharp downward tug. To onlookers, this seems like a rough procedure, but then they didn't have the same instructor that I did—a strong-minded aunt who came here on a visit from England. Walking around the garden with her, I was bemoaning my difficulties with seeding lavender. She stopped dead in her tracks and looked at me in astonishment. "Oh, for goodness' sake, pull yourself together, Elsa. This is what you do—" She bent over a large lavender and began ripping off sizable pieces. She jabbed them (I use the word advisedly, for she was cross with me) into the ground around the lavender plant and we moved on. She went back to England. Every one of her lavender cuttings lived, and I think of the border as hers.

I now realize that sharp tug makes a cutting with a "heel" of older wood, which roots well. So that's what I do. Ideally, in late June, before flowering (but often later), I tuck cuttings in around the big plant. Once or twice I've gone by the textbook, which involves preparing a bed in a part of the garden where the cuttings won't be

Fleshy stem cuttings from chrysanthemum root quickly and easily.

The "heel" seems to help rooting on the woody stems of lavender. It may still be twelve months or more before you get results.

Enjoy your work. Take a low stool into the garden and take the pain out of tedious jobs. Selecting lavender cuttings is best done before the flowers open.

disturbed, adding sharp sand to the soil, and even using a rooting hormone powder. Not to be scientific about it, I'd say roughly half the cuttings root successfully either way. I leave them in place until the following spring because the winter is too hard for them after transplanting.

Propagation by root cuttings is most often employed by commercial growers, who need large numbers of plants annually, and you may not find it too useful at this stage. I've grown good little oriental poppy plants from root cuttings, but I now leave this job to the mice, who over several winters have spread the beautiful pink 'Helen Elizabeth' poppy into some surprising places.

Some shrubs can be difficult for a home gardener to propagate by cuttings, but there is a method called layering, which I find almost magical. It has worked well for me on a number of shrubs, from very big rhododendrons to the fragrant little evergreen garland flower (*Daphne cneorum*). When layered, one shrubby cinquefoil (*Potentilla* 'Abbotswood') provided me with all the plants I can use and plenty more to give away. These and many other shrubs will sometimes layer themselves if they have branches or stems close to the ground, and if the over-zealous gardener doesn't cultivate or otherwise disturb the soil under them.

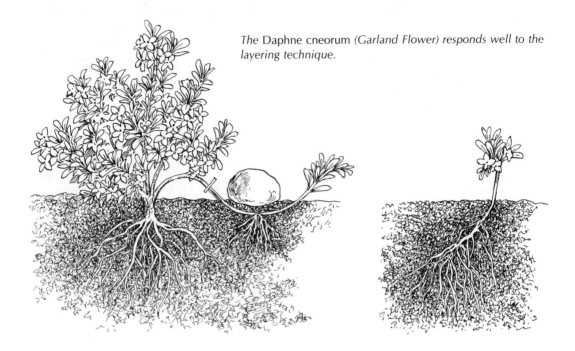

The Daphne cneorum (Garland Flower) responds well to the layering technique.

To layer, choose a likely looking branch as low on the shrub as possible. At a point halfway between the growing tip and where the branch arises, scrape the under surface to wound it a little—a fingernail is often enough. Lay it down on the ground, draw some soil over it, and hold it down by putting a flat stone on it (in my garden, there's always a stone within easy reach). Do this early in summer and allow it a whole season to put down roots. Once it has made sufficient roots, you can sever it from the mother plant. It is now on its own roots, but I like to leave it in place until the following spring, when it can be safely moved to its permanent location.

In these pages I have usually recommended spring as the best time for moving and dividing. This may be because I garden in the Northeast, but it's a safe time for most perennials, and obviously advisable for plants that bloom in late summer and fall. I like to divide standard border plants—phlox, delphinium, shasta daisies—as early in spring as I can; in fact, as soon as I see their green shoots. Helenium, boltonia, asters, and rudbeckias, and others that bloom later in summer and into fall, can be safely divided a little later.

Perennials that bloom early in spring—painted daisy, meadow rue, hardy geranium, lungwort—will look much better if division is done the year before. Fall is recommended as the "correct" time for this, but I do this successfully at various times over the summer, dividing when the plant has finished blooming.

Keep in mind that we want the plants in our garden to be at their best when they are in bloom. We should give them several months to establish themselves in their new, smaller size, so that they can look like real plants and not divisions at bloom time. In gardening, we should always be looking ahead (don't look back; something may be gaining on you, as Satchel Paige warned many years ago).

I want to pass on my experience with two widely grown perennials that are rapid multipliers and candidates for frequent divisions—daylilies and Siberian iris. They can be divided with safety at any time in the growing season, but I have found that the shape of the plant and quality of bloom are sometimes poor if they are not divided until the spring of the year. So catch these plants in fall.

I have to tell you, as I set down these rules, that I'm only too aware of breaking as many of them as I obey. Sometimes it's because I can't wait to see the effect of an idea I've just had; more often, it's because of the exigencies of time. You know what spring is like; one day the garden is too wet to venture onto it, and next day it's summer. Fall is not much better. There's frost. Then comes foliage time (which brings friends to stay). Thanksgiving is earlier every year, I swear. And suddenly it's all over. So, go by the rules whenever possible, and when it's not, do the best you can; you'll find out what works in your garden and what doesn't.

SAVING SEED

Seed saving is not generally recommended as a means of increasing perennials because so often they do not come true. But if this is not important, you may find yourself with some attractive variations. I have been very pleased with some of the results from open-pollinated delphinium and columbine.

I hold my breath every time the new catalogs come out, in case some annuals I particularly like have been dropped. So, out of anxiety, I often save seed of flowers such as love-in-a-mist (*Nigella damascena*), candytuft (*Iberis umbellata*), and certain annual poppies. They are too important to my summer color scheme for me to be without them.

Sowing Seeds Indoors

Raising seedlings indoors is an option. If you need only a few it's easy to find them ready-grown at the nursery. If you want them in numbers—and you do, I hope—it pays to buy seed and raise them yourself. (If you don't enjoy it, it doesn't pay, no matter how much less it costs.)

Buy good seeds. Read all you can about the many varieties and order early, as soon as the catalogs come in, because choice varieties sell out fast. If you have the seeds before the time is right for sowing, keep them in the refrigerator (not the freezer).

You will need:

- **Containers.** A few flats or plastic trays, no more than two to three inches deep. You can make this operation as simple or fancy as you wish. Cut-down milk containers and foil trays from coffee cakes and TV dinners used to be fine, but garden centers carry a wide range of containers and even complete starter kits. (Note: sterilize before reusing containers.)

- **Planting medium.** Unless you plan to grow on a large scale, I strongly recommend a commercial mix. I have had success with soilless Jiffy-Mix (principally peat moss and vermiculite, with some nutrients), but new products are coming out all the time, and brand names may change. The chief benefits are that the particles are of uniform size and the product is sterile—no weed seeds and a reduced chance of disease.

I suggest saving the seed heads on plants with the strongest form and from flowers of the most intense color. Be sure to leave them on the plant until they have fully ripened. Some seeds can be scattered on the ground after fall cleanup; others should be stored in a cool, dry, and dark place until the following spring. Label their containers. You think you'll remember what they are, but if you are at all like me, you won't.

- **Labels.** Some kind of labeling is essential, but there's no need to be fancy—this is a very temporary home for the seedlings. Three- to four-inch white plastic labels move easily in damp mix. Use a waterproof pen.

- **Water-soluble fertilizer.** This is necessary when seedlings are in a soilless mix. Use at half (or even less) the strength recommended on the container, and use at every watering once the true (recognizable) leaves appear.

Water and drain the mix before sowing. Sow as thinly as possible in shallow rows, marked by pressing lightly with the edge of a piece of wood (a pencil will do). Sprinkle a little dry mix over the seeds unless instructions say not to cover.

Germination can take place in anything from four or five days to two weeks or more. Keep the surface of the mix damp at all times. Once the first pair of leaves is visible, good light is a must. If you are growing under artificial lights this is taken care of, but on a sunny windowsill, for example, containers must be turned regularly or the seedlings will be lanky and will "lean" hopelessly in one direction. Seedlings should be "pricked out" into containers affording more space for each one. I use a coarser plant mix at this stage—usually ProGro.

After that, it's a matter of providing food and light until they can safely go outside to be hardened off before planting in the garden for bloom all summer.

See *The New Seed-Starter's Handbook* by Nancy Bubel.

CHAPTER 7

. . . .

HOW I PLANT

G ood planting means, first and foremost, meeting the plant's needs. This is easier to do if you have some knowledge of its habits and the conditions under which it has grown—or been grown—before coming into your hands. Over a number of years, my experience has led me to certain conclusions about how to handle the many different kinds of plants to be put into the garden.

Mail-order plants are in a class by themselves. Bare-root stock is no problem but some plants, especially those that have been dug in growth and shipped unpotted, need R and R as much as anything after three or four days in a closed container.

Larger plants growing in containers, bought locally, need more work before planting out than is generally recognized. After two years, the roots may be coiled round against the sides of the pot and must be pried loose before going into the ground.

First-year perennials and annual seedlings are easy to handle, but demanding of attention in their first few days out in the garden.

Least trouble of all are the perennial plants one moves from one part of the garden to another. Even so, there are strategies I have found to guarantee a smooth and painless move.

There is no need to be afraid of moving plants and I hope I can dispel any fear that you may have. A few successful moves, and you'll be so set up you'll be ready to tackle a delphinium in full spike. So here are my findings; they're not rules—they're what have worked for me.

*M*AIL-ORDER PLANTS

I'm going to start with how I handle mail-order plants because these are usually the first plants that I have to deal with in the year. I send the orders away any time in January or February (the catalogs come earlier every year, usually in December now). Unless you specify a certain date, the plants are likely to be shipped at the reasonable planting date in that nursery's area. For me, a reasonable date is about May 1, although if I'm buying from, say, South Carolina, their reasonable date is often a good deal earlier.

Mail-order nurseries ship their plants in the way best calculated to get them to the customer in good condition, so they may be bare-root, potted, or dug and wrapped. Consider first the plants that are shipped bare-root. These are totally dormant and have been held in cold storage since they were dug. They don't look too promising when you unpack them, these bare sticks, but the fact that the leaf buds have not opened is a plus—there will be no loss of moisture through the leaves. Many trees and shrubs, and quite a few perennials, especially roses, are shipped this way, and I've found that they grow well.

We'll assume that you have prepared a place for your plants ahead of time.

*A*SSEMBLING THE ELEMENTS

One thing I found out quite early on was that the best thing I could do for any plant was to give it a good footing in nutrient-rich soil. Which means compost. So, bearing that in mind, here is a list of things to have handy before starting to plant.

- Compost. "Handy" is an important word here. If the compost pile is far away you'll tell yourself that you can do without it "this time." But what a pity that would be, what a missed opportunity. You're going to be digging a hole anyway, so get some of this good stuff underneath the plant, where it will do the most good. Every hole should have compost in the bottom before you set the plant. (See *Compost*, page 43.)
- Tools: spade, trowel, small hand rake, clippers (see *Tools*, page 99).
- Soluble plant food and buckets, hose connected to water.
- Labels made for each plant.
- Stakes, brush, or other supports.
- Baskets or other covers to shade plants.
- The plants themselves—but leave them indoors or in the shade, out of sun and wind, until all preparations are complete.

For trees, it's a good idea to prepare a hole the previous fall (if your plans are made that far ahead) to allow the soil to settle over the winter. You should unwrap the package as soon as you receive it and soak the roots in water for an hour or two before planting. Evening is the preferred time for planting out, or at least after sundown. It gives the plants a night to recover. If, however, you can't plant that day, open the package and put it in a cool, dark place. It is not a good idea to soak roots any longer than the recommended time.

Now for the planting. Dig a generous hole, allowing width as well as depth. A common mistake is to make a deep, narrow hole. This puts the plant's roots down in cold soil without opportunity for lateral growth. Put your compost in and make a mound or cone in the center of the hole. Rest the base of the plant on this and spread the roots out and down all around the cone.

We'll take a rosebush for our example of bare-root planting. Hold the plant in one hand in such a way that when the hole is filled in the rose will be at the same level as it was before (you will usually see a line where the soil surface had been, but do read the instructions that come with the plants). Fill in with soil, firming it in between the roots with your fingers. If you find you've planted it too deeply, jiggle it up and down gently. If it seems to be too high, there's nothing for it but to redig the hole.

Once you are satisfied that the plant is at the right height, push the soil in around the roots and tamp down firmly. With a good-sized plant, you can use your feet. The "saucer" around the plant should be an inch or two lower than the surrounding soil so that the soil won't wash away when you water the plant.

Now stand back and look at the plant. Is it straight? Does it show its best face forward? At this stage—before it's been watered—you can still move the plant very easily. When you're satisfied with the position of the plant, it's time to water it in.

I like to use a hose to water because it supplies more force; this is not a time for gentle watering. The purpose is to force the soil down around the roots, leaving no air pockets, so direct a stream of water down around the plant. Once you have watered, do not tamp anymore or you will compress the wet soil. Permit the planting to drain completely and draw loose soil in over the surface. If it's still early in the spring, it's a good idea to hill the plant up slightly with loose soil or whatever mulch you have at hand. I use pine needles because they are airy (and because we have so many of them).

There's no need to prune rosebushes at this stage. Pruning will have been done at the nursery, but do remove any label that's wired onto the stem, or it will damage the plant as it grows.

Don't despair if nothing happens for a few weeks. When the leaf buds do "break," the whole plant will take off like a rocket. One year, I waited all through May—no sign of life; all through June—no sign of life. Came July, and the rose burst into leaf and then bloomed.

Mail-order nurseries also ship plants that are neither bare-root nor potted. These plants are at considerable risk because *they are not dormant.* They have been dug and interrupted in their growth. Nurseries must exercise the greatest care in packing them. I've received boxes of plants from the best—each plant, its roots holding a little ball of soil or planting mix, wrapped in damp newspaper, a name label attached, and the whole held tightly in two rubber bands. Lying on their side in a strong mailing carton, they are packed in wood shavings and the leafy tops are separated by pieces of rigid cardboard. Interestingly enough, these are not necessarily from nurseries with the highest prices. Once safely received these plants will ask more of you, also.

If such nondormant plants arrive before it is safe to plant them outside, you may have to pot them up yourself. I hate to do this because it's one more job in a busy spring, but it will hold them until

Planting a bare-root rose

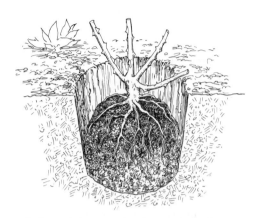

A. *Spread the roots out over a mound of compost or good soil.*

B. *Firm in, and water with force.*

C. *When drained, fill in with loose soil and mulch over crown.*

you can get them into the ground. Use a good planting mix such as ProGro. This commercial soilless mix is made up of roughly equal parts of peat moss and vermiculite. It holds moisture well and is sterile. Water the pots lightly and set them in a cool, shady place; after several days in a cardboard carton they cannot be expected to withstand wind or hot sun. Don't worry if some of the older leaves yellow and die; the plant will be making new leaves. Feed with a weak solution of soluble fertilizer when you put them out into the garden.

Mail-order plants that come in pots will generally be in good shape and can be left outside in their pots for a week or more until you are ready to plant them, but you must check daily to see if they need water.

Your job will be to make a smooth transition from pot to open ground. Take a plant, tip it out of its pot and see how the roots are growing. If they are clumped together, separate them. If they are long and wound around the root ball, clip some of them off. If it looks as if the plant has been in that pot for a considerable time, make several cuts with a knife down the sides of the root ball. The planting

After some time in the confines of a pot, the plant, like the aster shown here, may girdle itself with roots. Ease them free of the soil ball and spread out when planting.

procedure will be the same as for bare-root stock but, since these plants have leaves and could lose moisture through transpiration, you should provide some shade for them.

With all these planting procedures, one hopes for a calm and cloudy day, but sometimes you can wait no longer and have to risk planting under less than ideal conditions. No matter what type of plant you ordered, you should have the catalog at hand for reference. Nurseries are putting out better and better cultural notes with their plant orders, and you might as well read the instructions without waiting for the "if all else fails" part.

CONTAINER-GROWN PLANTS FROM LOCAL NURSERIES

In the Northeast, you can go to a local nursery by the end of April, beginning of May, and look for the perennials you want. Take your list, by all means, but keep an open mind in case you come across something else worthwhile. Go for tough, bushy, well-shaped plants. Never mind that they're not in flower—they shouldn't be at this time of year.

A local nurseryman decided to meet the demand for delphiniums; he seeded some in winter and put the individually potted plants on sale in May. They were handsome, bushy plants five or six inches tall, but they didn't sell. He realized why when a customer who asked for them took one look and said, "Oh, no. Delphiniums are five or six feet tall, with enormous blue spikes." Did she really think a six-foot, flower-topped giant would be growing in a little plastic pot? My heartfelt advice—be an informed gardener. Learn to recognize plants from their foliage and buy them when they're small.

When you get home from the nursery you can plant right away or leave them in their pots a day or two to acclimatize them to your garden. This is important to me because my garden is on an exposed hillside at an elevation of eighteen hundred feet, whereas the nurseries that grew the plants are in a sheltered valley.

Compost at hand, you're ready to plant. Dig the hole and put the obligatory shovelful of compost in the bottom. Tip the plant out of its pot. Never pull the plant by its stem. You may have to knead the pot to loosen the plant. You can do this with your hands, or feet in the case of a large plant.

Most likely the plant will have been in that pot over winter and will fall out in a solid pot-shaped ball. Break up this ball, shorten extra-long roots, and be sure that no one root is girdling the others. Loosen the soil at the bottom of the root mass, and plant as described for bare-root plants.

Don't be afraid to treat the plant in this way. A healthy plant will soon grow more roots, and thrive. A new gardener's inclination is to plant the whole root mass undisturbed, but this can result in the weakening and eventual death of the plant as it is strangled by its own roots.

Occasionally, when you tip the pot upside down, instead of a pot-shaped ball of roots a whole potful of loose planting mix may fall out, revealing a scarcely rooted and pitifully small plant. This is because it has been sold too soon, so recently potted that it has not had time to root itself. (This often happens with plants that are the "in" thing that season, and the rush was not anticipated.) The only thing you can do is repot the plant, give it time to root and establish itself, then put it out in the ground and hope for the best.

*F*IELD-DUG PLANTS

These are larger plants and in general don't pose any difficulties. The grower will dig the plant, but is none too anxious to give you much soil with it. On one occasion an enthusiastic young man working at the nursery shook a plant vigorously. "Don't want all that dirt on it, do we?" he said. "Yes, we do," I said, and left him holding it.

When you buy a field-dug plant wrap it tightly in newspaper to hold it together on the journey home. It's possible that it may not have been growing in the best soil, and if so you should compensate by lining the planting hole with extra compost and by being generous with watering. One last thing: check to see if there are weeds in the root mass; these may be small, but they're ambitious. Getting them out now is easy; later, much harder.

*T*RANSPLANTING SMALL SEEDLINGS

The seedlings you buy from nurseries and farmers' markets are most likely to be annuals growing in plastic packs. The method of planting depends on whether you want a mass of a certain annual in the border or whether you want a row of them in a cutting garden or some out-of-the-way part of your property.

If you have to hold them for a day or two before planting, you must be scrupulous about watering. I water from the bottom by setting them in a larger tray partly filled with water, lifting them out when I see the surface of the soil turn dark with moisture. Watering from above, I have lost some seedlings because the taller plants prevented the water from reaching the shorter ones. Remember the weak solution of plant food every time you water.

If you grew your own seedlings, you will probably have them in greater numbers than if you're buying six-packs from the nursery. Whether you grew them under lights in a basement, in a greenhouse, or on a kitchen windowsill, outdoor conditions are going to be a shock to them. Take time to "harden them off" gradually.

I have a special warning about seedlings in peat pots. I know the promotional material for these peat pots claims "no root shock," but I'd rather risk the shock than plant it pot and all and have the peat wall dry up so that the roots cannot penetrate it. If you do plant them in their pots, soak the whole thing thoroughly before putting it in the ground and be sure none of the peat wall is left above ground, for it will act as a wick and draw out all the moisture.

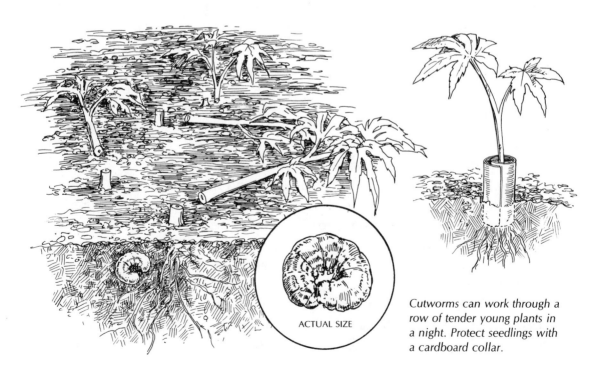

ACTUAL SIZE

Cutworms can work through a row of tender young plants in a night. Protect seedlings with a cardboard collar.

While I'm playing Cassandra, let me give you one more warning: watch out for cutworms. These miserable little caterpillars can demolish a planting overnight by nipping off the tender stems at soil level, leaving them lying on the ground. Small and therefore tender plants seem to be their favorites, and the greatest danger is in the first few days after planting out. I once lost a whole row of six-inch delphinium seedlings before waking up to the cause of the danger. Not anymore, I may say.

Seek and destroy is your mission. It's not difficult, because by day cutworms lie curled, gray and horrid, just below the surface of the soil, waiting for nighttime. They do not move far from the tender seedlings. By the time you find them they will have done the damage, so prevention is better. Put a small cardboard collar around the base of each plant to deter the varmints.

Moving Plants Around in Your Own Garden

This is the most fun for me, and I do a lot of it. There are all sorts of valid reasons for moving a plant. It may be growing too big and need to be moved further back. It may be a frail plant being overshadowed. It may be too similar in leaf texture to its neighbor. It may bloom at the wrong time for its companion plant. It may turn out to have an impossible flower color.

Whatever the reason, you're in charge, so go ahead and move it. Think of the operation not so much as digging a plant but moving a sizable chunk of garden with that plant in it. You will increase your chances of success if you can plan to get the idea one day and move it the next. This enables you to water it the night before the move. Damp soil holds together better than dry.

Next day, dig a suitable hole and half fill it with compost. Now dig your plant in its chunk of soil, carry it carefully on a spade, and lower it into the prepared hole. This time do not disturb the root ball. Put loose soil into any visible cracks, and firm until you cannot see the outline of the transplant. Water thoroughly but gently with a slow trickle from the hose. In all likelihood that plant won't know it's been moved.

On one or two occasions I've had to move plants without any of the valid reasons I've listed. Two large and sportive dogs had chased a chipmunk into a flower border that I had primped and plumped for a Significant Occasion in a client's garden, three miles away. The delphiniums were the first to go, their hollow, five-foot stalks snapping off below the flower spikes.

I dug three from my own garden, wrapped each huge root ball in plastic, and splinted the long flower stems with thin bamboo. I laid them down flat in the back of my small station wagon, and with the gate open drove the three miles in twenty minutes. And, at six in the morning, in a fine mist, I put them in beside the broken ones. The mist cleared. The sun came out. The Occasion was a great success.

When it was over I brought them home in the dusk and replanted them. One had distinct curvature of the flower spike, but next morning all were fine and remained so.

I would have liked to boast, but couldn't do so without ever after being suspected of garden fakery.

PLANTS WITH SPECIAL REQUIREMENTS

Peonies and poppies, two of the outstanding plants of the June garden, must be planted at the end of the season instead of the beginning. (As I have suggested elsewhere in these pages, it is best to order from nurseries that have made a specialty of these plants.)

Oriental poppy roots are shipped from August on, when the plants are dormant; they do not survive handling at any time of year when in active growth. The actual planting method is the same as for most perennials, but this plant is different in that soon after planting (even if it is as late as October-November) it sends up a rosette of leaves. These form a living mulch that serves to protect the plant from winter damage. It's still a good idea to mulch the crown, but be careful to ease the mulching material *under the leaves.* Those leaves will die away in spring, when new growth begins.

A mature oriental poppy can occupy a space two to three feet in diameter. After blooming, the plant goes dormant, dying back to the soil line and leaving a large, awkward space in the border, so plant late summer perennials near it, or be prepared to put annuals in each year.

Peony roots are shipped later, usually from October on, and very strange-looking they are when you unpack them. I've had numerous telephone calls from gardeners familiar with the growing plant but seeing the underground part for

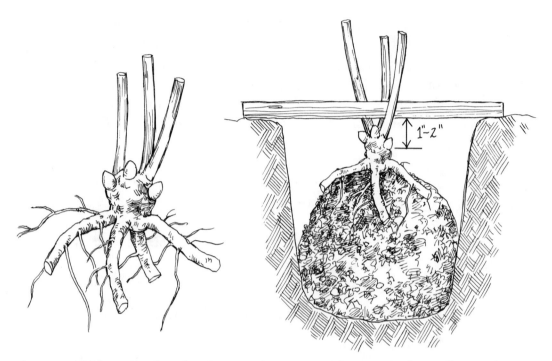

The peony root that arrives from the nursery can be a strange sight to new gardeners. Once you've established which way is up, remember the most important thing—pink buds must be no deeper than two inches below the soil surface. Placing a stick across the top of the hole will make your measuring more accurate.

the first time. It's hard to know which way is up; the cut-back stubs of the past season's stems often are assumed mistakenly to be cut-off roots, and the unfortunate peony gets planted upside down. It might survive, but why make its life more difficult than it need be?

Peony plants are long-lived (there have been a few hundred-year-old plants on record!). Unlike many other perennials, peonies don't take easily to being moved, so you will need to make the best possible home for them.

There is one absolute rule: a peony must be planted with the pink bud (leaf bud not flower) *no deeper than one to two inches* below the surface of the soil. Any deeper and, although you may get a fine display of foliage, there will be no flowers.

Set the peony on a mound of soil in a generous-sized hole. Lay a long stick across the top of the hole to make it easier to see that the buds are at the right depth. With your fingers, keep adding and firming soil around the roots. Water thoroughly but not so vigorously that the plant sinks below the desired level. You may mulch for the first winter to prevent the soft soil from heaving, but after that the peony is on its own; it can take—in fact, needs—deep winter cold in order to bloom well.

Animal manures are not recommended when planting peonies because of the risk of disease, but bone meal is a valuable, slow-acting additive. A warning here: put the bone meal well down in the ground, don't sprinkle it on the surface. Dogs love it; they think it's an old stinky bone and once they get the scent will dig up your newly planted peony.

Those are the basics of planting as I practice it; you will no doubt develop some tricks and techniques that work for you. But there is no need to be daunted by the process. The right tools can make any planting job easier.

Tools

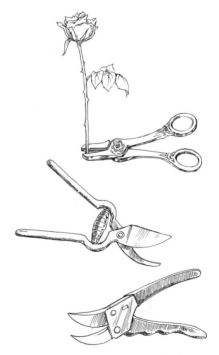

The choice of tools is a highly personal one, and in the end whatever you find easiest to work with will probably be the best tool for the job. Nevertheless I'm going to give you a list of fifteen tools that I use regularly in my own garden because they work well and add pleasure to the job, and I would like you to have the same pleasure.

This doesn't mean you have to rush out and buy all of them immediately. There are some you won't need for a season or two and some that will double for others. A few of them may not be for you at all. Cut-and-hold flower scissors, for instance, that need one outstretched hand only, enable me to cut and deadhead flowers without falling into the border. You may get more fun than I do out of

More cutting tools. At top: A clever tool often called "cut-and-hold" and most useful on flowers.

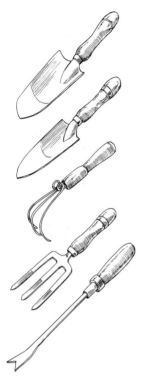

Beyond the obvious hand trowels and hand forks, there are tools for clawing out debris under plants, and—to me—an indispensable deep weeder for dandelion roots.

crawling under shrubs to get out dead leaves, in which case you won't need the claw cultivator. I use a pitchfork to lift big piles of compost, but you may do as I did for years and use your regular garden fork.

Unfortunately, the most essential tools, like the spade and border fork, are the ones that are going to cost the most, and in my opinion you cannot economize on either. I went through any number of inexpensive ones in short order before I found the ones that I have been working with now for over ten years (and expect to use for another ten). Most of the tools on the list are standard and available anywhere, but two of them are not. I'm suggesting them to you here because, in my garden, helpers and students alike have been so taken with them that they have bought their own and abandoned their old ones.

One of the special tools is the Dutch hoe. Some years ago, when I couldn't find one in this country, I had to bring one from England. I'm glad to see now that it is listed in several catalogs, sometimes as "Dutch scuffle hoe."

I don't get along well with hoes in general, but this one is a real pleasure to use. To begin with, you don't have to keep lifting it up, hacking and chopping down (impossible in a flower border, anyway) and filling your boots with earth. It's a push hoe, and you "scuffle," with the blade no more than an inch or two below

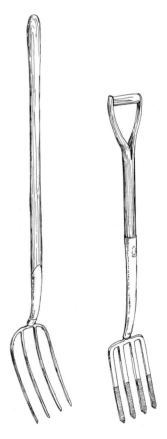

Left: *Pitchfork*   Right: *Border fork*

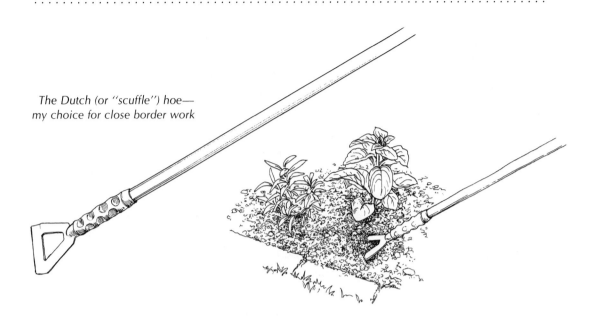

*The Dutch (or "scuffle") hoe—
my choice for close border work*

the soil's surface and parallel to it. There's less wear and tear on both the gardener and the plants.

The second special tool is the border fork, more often called a spading fork in this country. But, being designed for use in close flower plantings, it is smaller and narrower, and I have yet to see it in stores. The stainless-steel head with four tines, and the plastic-coated D-grip handle make it an unbeatable tool. So far, the only forks constructed like this that are available here are British-made (no chauvinism, I assure you). This tool, with others of similar quality (including stainless-steel hand tools and a stainless-steel Dutch hoe), appears in many catalogs. The tools are expensive so it pays to do some comparison shopping among the catalogs.

When you look at the first two tools on the list, you'll see that I make a distinction between *spade* and *shovel* and their respective functions. Digging, which involves cutting down into the soil, often through turf, is most efficiently done with a *spade*, which has a straight and sharp cutting edge. The *shovel* is best used for scooping up and carrying soil, manure, and gravel, for example. It makes an inefficient digging tool. Calling each by its right name might begin to put things straight.

Digging with a spade

Top: *Grass shears*　Bottom: *Loppers*

I don't offer detailed advice on such items as wheelbarrows or garden carts—I know you won't be gardening very long before you realize you're spending a lot of time and muscle just getting things from here to there, and you won't do without them. What I will tell you is that the most pricey are not necessarily the best.

Don't buy a wheelbarrow unless its balance (and yours) is excellent, and don't buy the biggest garden cart in the store or catalog unless it comes with the pony or donkey required to pull it when loaded. Several lightweight, less expensive and probably short-lived carts (though I have a veteran that's twenty years old and still sturdy), will be more useful. It's funny how you always need one more wheelbarrow, cart, or whatever it is, so do yourself a favor and get it.

Neither am I about to go into the myriad accessories in stores and catalogs, some useful, some less useful: a tarpaulin, for sliding heavy plants from one place to another; hoses, buckets, and watering cans; compost thermometers, rain gauges, plant supports and twine; plant labels, hanging baskets, fertilizers, boots and boot scrapers; gardeners' gloves, knee pads and kneeling mats; Sussex trugs; trellises, bowers, pillars, gazebos, and the odd Greek temple.

I am reminded of a modest little establishment in England many years ago, where my father bought his seeds, chicken grain, and, once a year, live chicks. I remember the gloomy interior, its musty smell, and the chaff that made me sneeze. Over the door, in fancy letters, was a sign: "Corn Chandler, Seedsman, Purveyor of Sundries." What couldn't that proprietor have done with all these sundries!

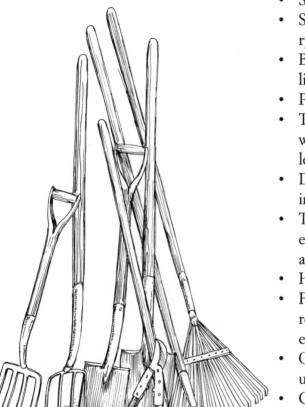

MY TOOLS:

- Spade, sharp-edged, for digging;
- Shovel, for picking up and carrying soil, manure, etc.;
- Border fork (spading fork), for lighter digging and border work;
- Pitchfork (compost fork);
- Two rakes, steel-toothed, for soil; wire-toothed, for grass and leaves;
- Dutch hoe for weeding and aerating in the borders;
- Two or three hand trowels, different sizes and shapes, for planting and weeding;
- Hand fork, for small weeds;
- Forked deep weeder, for taprooted weeds like dandelions, etc.;
- Claw cultivator, for cleaning up under shrubs;
- Grass shears;
- Heavy shears, for clipping and pruning;
- Long-handled lopping shears, for tougher pruning jobs;
- Hand pruner (clipper);
- Flower cutters, cut-and-hold type.

One day's work in my garden can call for this range of tools.

CHAPTER 8

. . . .

SHAPING THE GARDEN

S ay the word "border," and the picture that most often comes to mind is of long, deep flower beds backed by high walls of rosy brick or venerable hedges of yew. This, of course, is the romantic view, and has much to do with perceptions of the grand and glorious herbaceous borders created around the turn of the century.

Today, surviving examples in England, most of them now maintained by the National Trust, draw visitors in the hundreds of thousands. I have to smile when I remember how small versions of borders in modest suburban gardens were elevated by their proud owners to the full rank of The Herbaceous Border.

In general, "border" is taken to mean any long flower bed usually, but not necessarily, bordering a path, a driveway, an outer edge of the garden. A bed is a more or less free-standing area; island beds, set down in lawn, may have any shape at all. Borders or beds, the possible forms they may take are infinite, ranging from great double flower borders to small plantings of two or three perennials in a dooryard bed. There are as many ways of planting as there are people who grow flowers.

I have been blessed with the opportunity to "mess about" in my garden, to make my own mistakes, come to my own conclusions, arrive at my own style— all before reading and hearing what were the "right" and "wrong" things to do. What I fervently wish for you is the same sort of experience that I had—to make your own mistakes and arrive at your own style. I hope that long before you finish reading this you'll be making your own discoveries—different places for flower beds, new arrangements of plants, lovely flower combinations not described in any book.

The question of where to grow your flowers is an important one. I've already uttered warnings about "setting down imperatives, holding hope in the back of your mind, and, for the time being, putting realities first," but I think they bear repeating.

First you're going to use whatever landscape or man-made feature there is to plant against. For a long border, you might use a wall, a fence, the side of an interesting outbuilding. For a free-standing bed you might have something to plant around, perhaps an interesting old tree, a large rock outcropping, a wellhead. If you fail to find any of these or similar promising backgrounds and plan to make a bed that stands on its own, stop and think carefully.

On esthetic grounds, of course, I have an objection to dotting the garden with little blobs of color, but I know the irresistible urge to take the spade and chop into the lawn to make a flower bed. Then you see another perfect spot for flowers and you chop out another. Only a small one, you rationalize to yourself.

I would like to make a dampening observation here. I'm acutely conscious of edges (that's where the planted bed meets the grass). Edges and failure to keep them up have been the undoing of a number of beginning gardeners. Take a look at how much edging care you'll end up with and see if it is in reasonable proportion to the area you'll have for flowers. You may get a surprise. Two small beds, five feet by two feet each, will give you a total area of twenty square feet for flowers, and an edging total of twenty-eight running feet. One larger bed, seven by three feet, gives a growing area of twenty-one square feet for only twenty feet of edging. Just thought I'd mention it.

Wherever you put a flower bed, try to make it look as if it had grown out of its surroundings, and not as if it had been dropped onto the garden from above. You can help to achieve this effect by "anchoring" a bed at one end to a small tree, large shrub, perhaps a rock outcropping, or by wrapping it around a low bank or other change in ground level. If even that fails you, look further away, find a line of trees or a boundary of sorts and echo it by repeating its curve in your border.

CURVED OR STRAIGHT?

I'm often asked whether I think straight lines or curved are better for beds and paths. The answer is that in the right place one is no more "right," meaning esthetically pleasing, than the other. The important thing is that there should be good reason for the choice, and this will usually be suggested by the setting.

*A small tree or a rock outcropping can make a
flower bed look as if it belongs in the landscape.*

People have an idea that a curved line is intrinsically more "artistic" than a straight line. This was certainly true of a neighbor of mine. We were walking around her newly laid out garden one day. Every edge in it was scalloped, like bed linen. Curves billowed out to meet other curves instead of appearing to fit gently into one another; in several places they reduced the grass walk between them to an impossible twelve inches.

A rooftop view in spring reveals the combination of curved and straight lines in the garden.

While I tried to compose a suitable remark, one that wouldn't lose me a friend for life, she looked at me anxiously. "Is it too much?" she asked. Coward that I was, I murmured, "A little." But when she said she thought another "meandering path" would be nice, my heart sank. Ye gods, I thought, one more wavy line wobbling off into the distance! But we came to a peaceful accommodation and were able to laugh about it later. When I asked her why all the curves, she said

Some borders echo the contours of the surrounding landscape—the ellipse of the pond and the drive curving around the trees.

she thought it was more artistic. It wasn't the first time I'd heard that offered as a reason for choosing curved lines over straight.

As a general rule, formal beds, rectilinear in shape, look "right" with formal or classic architecture; informal (and therefore probably curved) flower beds look "right" with an informal house. Doubtless this is another oversimplified rule, for I have seen it wonderfully and daringly broken.

The landscape surrounding the garden at Heath is beautiful; it is also overwhelming. It wasn't until I took a look from the roof of the house that I knew my flower beds and borders had to be in harmony with the gentle contours surrounding them. Everywhere I looked there were curves: sloping meadows falling gently away from the house; an oval pond with its "picket fence" of white birch trees; to the north behind it, a series of hills; and to the east, more folded hills stretching to a mountain sixty miles away. Even the old cart track up to the sugarbush (now the driveway to the house) made a beautiful curve, winding around between the pond and a copse of maple and birch. The only boundary close enough to hold on to was a woodland, stopping short at an old stone wall running down the south side of the garden. So my flower beds took their shapes, lying in harmony with these forms, each curving to repeat the contour of the landscape beyond it.

In such an open, exposed garden, a small pathway to a green square helps to give some sense of entry and enclosure.

SEEING THE GARDEN IN A DIFFERENT WAY

Once when I was completely stumped for a solution to a problem, I walked past the house and looked in the big windows that face the garden. The sun was in such a position that instead of seeing the room inside I had a perfect picture of the entire garden, but in reverse. I was transfixed. It looked so much better, so much more interesting, and as I stared I saw just exactly what I should do.

Now I take a big old-fashioned hand mirror and look at gardens in reflection. You might try it for an entirely new perspective that enables you to take a fresh run at such problems as where to place a bed, or a path, or a tree.

If I could wish myself back thirty years, knowing how involved I would become with gardening, I would let flowers and flower beds wait (but how could I? It was flowers I wanted); I would put my worldly goods up for sale and buy trees of all kinds, in generous number and of good size, and let them frame out a garden of more reasonable proportions.

But as it is, much of my garden is seen against an extraordinary background, if you can call it that. I didn't plant it, it requires no upkeep, it can change color several times a day, and I think it will be there forever. The great bowl of sky over my garden is both joy and trial. Many of my flowers have to be very tall and very bold to be seen to advantage against such a sweep of sky.

In only one part of the garden, where a flower bed is backed by the woods and a stone wall to the south, are plants seen against anything resembling a conventional background. Here I recognized that some transition was needed from the natural landscape of woodland to the unnatural, that is, the cultivated landscape, my garden.

After a number of experiments in the "transition" bed, I finally came up with a planting that satisfied me. The side of this bed nearest the edge of the woods is straight and parallel to the woods. There I put native plants like joe-pye weed, angelica, doll's-eyes, and obedient plant. Among them, tall foxgloves send up their white flower spikes each spring, to echo in color and form the white birches at

the woodland edge. Just over that wall, I planted more foxgloves and doll's-eyes among the ferns, implying a question—have woodland plants wandered into the garden, or have some of the garden plants escaped to the woods?

In a garden with so many curves, I felt the need for one or two more straight lines. I had long promised myself a grass walk between planted borders, to terminate at the dark woods, and finally I fulfilled it. There's a special pleasure in the gradual unfolding—almost unrolling—of this border composition, offering a fresh picture with every step.

*S*TONE WALLS

If you are fortunate enough to have an old stone wall running along one edge of your garden, consider yourself among the luckiest of gardeners, with a ready-made background for a long perennial border. If you're not that fortunate, and you have a garden full of old stones that no one has yet seen fit to organize into a wall, how about doing it yourself? I understand wall-building is a peaceful, calming occupation with philosophic overtones, but I wouldn't presume to go into the business here of instructing anyone in how to build a wall. There are excellent books on the subject.

My husband, who is no gardener but an enthusiastic supporter, made a stone wall for me soon after I started the garden at Heath. The supply of stones was no problem; I unearthed one every time I dug a hole. The wall was about fifty feet long and, wherever it didn't fall down, about two and a half feet high (it fell down at any height greater than that).

There is one drawback to a lovely wall, however. Every lily bulb in that first border disappeared, the fibrous roots of the Siberian iris were chewed up into nests, and the pencil-thin roots of the oriental poppy were so widely distributed by mice that little plants came up in any number of unexpected places. Few backgrounds for perennials are as lovely as stone walls, but with walls, come mice, and one must make a choice. Robert Burns may have been right about "the best laid schemes of mice and men . . ." but clearly it's the men's (and women's) schemes that "gang aft agley"—the mice seem to be doing all right.

*T*RUST YOUR EYE

You will find several border designs in this book. Initially, I had not intended to include any because I didn't want you to follow a plan and miss the pleasure of putting your individual stamp on a garden of your own designing. Then I remembered that you could very well be starting from the ground up and might be more alarmed than excited at the prospect.

So there are some designs, after all. Just to get you started, you understand. I fully expect you to change things around after the first season; I'd be disappointed if you didn't.

I make countless planting plans for my own garden, although I rarely follow any of them. I don't consider this time wasted, however; making designs in the winter months is pure pleasure. As I write each plant name, I see the color of the flower, feel the texture of its leaves, and, for a moment, catch its scent. On a gray January day, what a trip that is!

In the garden itself, I most often create the border design as I go along. This is not as haphazard as it sounds. Whether consciously or not, much of what I do—where I put this plant, where that one—is guided by several things: information received from reading; personal experience gained over the years; but most of all, I think, by my eye, and what it tells me at the moment. That's why I hope it will be *your* eye, and nobody else's, that will direct your planting.

Gardens are marvelous places for expanding our powers of seeing. Trust your eye. This does not mean that you should disregard every scrap of conventional wisdom. The trouble is that a lot of good advice ends up in rigid columns—"thou shalt" and "thou shalt not"—because it's simpler that way. It's too complicated to add all the modifiers—"nevertheless in certain situations . . ." "Remember, however, that in some cases . . ." and so on.

Elsewhere in these pages I have said that good planting requires knowledge of the plant and its needs. That remains true whatever plans you have in mind for the plant. Think of its height, form (overall shape), foliage texture, flower form, flower color, time of bloom, hardiness, light and moisture requirements. Those are the obvious considerations. You will find answers to most of them in a catalog description or—in briefer form—on a plant tag in the pot. But it is your own experience that will so greatly enrich this basic information. Record it if you can; there is no substitute for it.

*P*LACING THE PLANTS

I began the list of considerations with *height*, because the basic border commandment relating to height is a perfect example of oversimplification. It's the one that says tallest at the back, shortest at the front (and guess where plants of middle height go). Slavish adherence to that maxim would result in an arrangement like a school photo—tall children standing at the back, middle row sitting on benches, front row cross-legged on the ground, the group usually flanked by two teachers, one at each end of the back row (for discipline or symmetry, one wonders?).

That is a photo; this is a garden. The photo is looked at from one angle, head-on; every child must be visible (or some parents would want their money back), but we're thinking here of a garden and of people moving about in it. The special pleasure of a long border is that as you walk along the path beside it, you see a changing picture with every step.

Height

You don't want to be conscious of how the plants are arranged; all you want is the impression of a community of flowers, beautifully and naturally grouped. Of course you're going to be guided to some extent by relative height; you wouldn't plant a solid clump of three-foot phlox in front of a delicate columbine only fourteen inches high. But there's a lot more to placing a plant than knowing how tall it is.

You need to consider what a plant's height consists of. Compare, for example, two late-summer beauties, both of which could legitimately be listed in a catalog as "tall, 5 feet." *Boltonia asteroides* 'Snowbank' is a dense five-foot mass of foliage and flowers; the five-foot daylily (*Hemerocallis altissima*) has a basal fountain of leaves no more than two feet high, and it is only the flowers on their long wiry stems that get up to five feet. Consideration of height alone would suggest the same place in the border for these two, but if you visualize them you will see that their form is every bit as important as their actual height in deciding where to place them.

Now think of some tall plants with delicate flowers and picture them not to the rear of the bed but right down at the front, to give the border an extra dimension. I like to use Russian sage (*Perovskia atriplicifolia*) in this way, also some of the tallest coralbells (*Heuchera sanguinea*) because both have airy movement in the slightest breeze, and have flowers and stems insubstantial enough to reveal other plants behind them. These delicate plants can do a lot for such sturdy but

Sturdy sweet William plants are glimpsed through a veil of airy coral bells.

prosaic midborder plants as perennial cornflower, sweet William, and Canterbury bells, which gain a little poetry when glimpsed through the veils.

And what about the short plants, so often automatically placed at the front of the border? Is height—or lack of it—the sole criterion? Again, I think form is just as important. As I write, I'm visualizing a part of the front of my border that I find especially pleasing. There are little mounds of thrift (*Armeria maritima*) and small cushions of 'Silver Mound' (*Artemisia schmidtiana* 'Nana') softening a front edge that would otherwise be uncompromisingly straight.

Plants which, though short, do not have this rounded plump shape are not nearly as attractive in this position. There is a dwarf balloon flower, 'Apoyama', a mere nine inches tall, whose height certainly qualifies it for the front, and a dwarf phlox, 'Pinafore Pink', that's even shorter, yet their form is wrong. Each of these plants carries its flowers on what looks like a bunch of stiff, erect stems, and neither does what I want for that front edge. But a much bigger plant—*Nepeta* × *faassenii* 'Six Hills Giant'—does. This big catmint, thirty inches or taller, planted in an awkward place where there is a ninety-degree corner to the border, billows out, turns the corner, as it were, and effectively conceals the sharp angle. The eye notes, and the mind receives with pleasure, the small surprise occasioned by the change in height.

Low mounding plants soften a border's hard, straight edge.

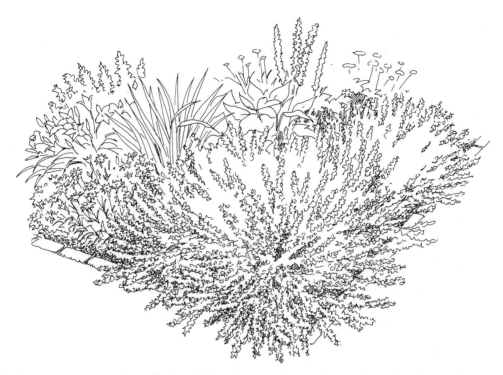

The big catmint Nepeta 'Six Hills Giant' billows over and conceals an awkward 90-degree corner.

Form

Every so often I grow something I can't resist, even though I know it's risky because of my garden's location, at the extreme limit of the plant's hardiness. *Gaura lindheimeri* and *Salvia grandiflora pitcheri* are two such plants. They come through the winter most years, but mine certainly aren't as handsome as the ones I've seen growing in Zone 6 and higher. In addition, and perhaps for the same reason, neither has particularly attractive foliage, but I grow both because I've found a perfect role for them.

Tucked in among stronger, bolder plants, their flowers seem to come from nowhere. The stems are long wands that wave over the tops of other plants, their small blossoms looking more like tiny moths or butterflies than flowers. I plant them so that the salvia's rich blue flowers hover over silvery pink Japanese anemones, to make a charming color combination. The pink-and-white gaura blossoms fluttering over the solid, bronze-red flower heads of the big stonecrop, 'Autumn Joy', offer not only pleasing color but interesting play between the delicate and the sturdy flower forms. I get the same pleasure when I see single baby's breath frothing around a strong double orange daylily.

Reaction to the interplay between delicate and strong elements in the border is one illustration of how much more than the eye is involved when we look at plants in a garden. Take, for instance, the strong response we have to different textures. We respond to prickly, angular plants like sea holly in quite a different way than we do to a soft and feathery plant like 'Silver Mound' artemisia. Without bending down to touch, we know what each would feel like.

*B*EYOND COLOR

To illustrate how I feel about the relative importance of form and color, visualize a bed of flowers in perfect color harmony, ranging perhaps from a palest pink to a deep violet, and planted exclusively with tall border phlox. They will all be of the same shape, with heavy trusses of flowers held at approximately the same height. The flowers and their colors are very beautiful but, to my mind, the picture is a little boring. Color has been taken care of, form neglected.

Three plants here present a sharp contrast in textures: Iris pallida 'Variegata'; Euphorbia polychroma; *and, behind them,* Coreopsis verticillata 'Golden Shower'.

Now substitute for some of the phlox a few plants with flowers in spires. These could be Kansas gayfeather (*Liatris spicata*), say, or the tallest astilbe (*Astilbe taquetii* 'Superba')—in the same color harmony but now with contrast in form. The border comes alive and piques your interest.

Take another example, this one a border later on in the season. Here there is a mix of traditional seasonal colors, from cream and palest yellow, through gold, to a rich bronze. Picture this planted with varieties of coreopsis, black-eyed Susans, marigolds, and chrysanthemums. All are similar; they are bushlike in form and have flowers of daisy type. How much more interesting it would be to vary this, to have, for example, a late snakeroot (*Cimicifuga simplex* 'The Pearl'), holding its white spires erect behind the compact, mounded black-eyed Susan (*Rudbeckia fulgida* 'Goldsturm'), and Canadian burnet (*Sanguisorba canadensis*) rising behind the cushions of chrysanthemums.

I find almost any combination of spires and mounds irresistible. But these are far from being the only shapes to play against one another. Think of them as spires, and torches, spikes, wands; mounds and cushions; climbers and weavers; clouds and veils; mats and carpets; as canopies and umbrellas. All this, in plants that range from the diminutive Johnny-jump-ups to a giant nine-foot angelica.

Granted, much of this is subliminal in effect, but it contributes to the total pleasurable experience. Our senses are able to take in so much more than we have words for, and every walk through the garden offers a gift to the senses.

And so we have come, at last, to what inspired you to make a garden in the first place—the flowers. Say what you will about all the other elements, flowers mean color. Even though plants are in leaf for a long season and in flower for only a small part of it, those flowers are the exquisite decorations of the border. After the carefully considered language used to evaluate plant form and leaf texture, sobriety flies out the window when we come to these miracles. Flowers like trumpets and bells, like goblets, pincushions, lockets, shells, and stars; flowers clustered into globes, candelabra, tassels, pagodas. And their colors!

When I stand before the border, one of these miracles in my hand, color, form, texture—all of this is in my mind. And then I know where I shall put it. "How very unscientific," you say, "suppose I do that and it's wrong—then what?" But you won't get it wrong. You're not in a world of right and wrong; you're in your garden and all you're looking for is your own ideal.

CHAPTER 9

....

COLOR IN THE GARDEN

*T*hat first year at Heath I planted annuals. Opening up a piece of garden as late as the end of May, I had to be content with whatever was left at local nurseries. I remember only too well what I found: petunias, mostly purple, red, and white; giant zinnias in every color; and a great array of marigolds of every size but only two colors—yellow and orange.

Faced with the same prospects today, I don't know what I would do, but back then I was made of sterner stuff. Wherever I could get a rock out I pushed a plant in, and then I went hunting for more annual seeds. I don't remember the total haul, but I know it included sunflowers ("Giant Russian Mammoth," it said on the packet), snapdragons, gloriosa daisies, nasturtium, hollyhocks, Siberian wallflower, and—is it possible I couldn't tell perennials from annuals?—oriental poppies ("Mixed Colors," the packet announced).

I recite this poverty-stricken list to give you some idea of the extraordinary wash of color that surrounded me that August. The nasturtiums took off, and their flowers covered the ground and the grass all around them in yellow and flame and bronze. Right next to them the sunflowers went up and up, their great shaggy gold heads eight feet or more in the air (tallest at the back, shortest in front? There was no back, no front). The stems grew so thick and strong that they had to be chopped down with an ax the next spring.

The hollyhocks got up to two inches and were eaten. The snapdragons never made an appearance. I swear, every seed of the oriental poppy (Mixed Colors) germinated, and after a year or two I had a long row of pure coral poppies. I enjoyed them for several seasons, until I decided I needed my colors more mixed than "Mixed Colors" had given me.

The gloriosa daisies and Siberian wallflowers germinated at what seemed like

150 percent and burst into electrifying orange flowers that bloomed right through until frost. I greeted everything with astonishment and gratitude; I'm happy to tell you I loved it all. I wince now when I think of that riot of yellow and orange, yet in a way it was exactly right. What hope would there have been for little flowers of modest color surrounded (and nearly overrun) as they would have been by the encroaching wildness, which had its own yellow and orange flowers— black-eyed Susans, goldenrod, and seeding grasses?

By the following year I was planting perennials in a bigger and better-prepared area. For the first time, I had the chance to buy full-sized plants and experiment with their placement in a long border. As a result of determined mowing, the grass around the border had begun to take on the appearance of a lawn—nothing special, you understand, but distinct at least from the wilderness around it. I no longer needed the giant yellow flowers of the previous year, though I still had plenty and to spare. Of the clumps of pass-alongs, too many, like coreopsis, helenium, and heliopsis, were of the yellow daisy persuasion. In addition, the previous year's gloriosa had seeded mightily.

ALL YELLOWS ARE NOT CREATED EQUAL

I was buying and planting delphinium, rosy coneflowers, phlox, globe thistles, anthemis, and yarrows of various colors. I was having a wonderful time trying out color compositions, but already I realized that many of the yellows looked brash and hardly any of them looked right with my other colors. I had been so sure a golden marguerite *Anthemis tinctoria* 'Kelwayi' would pair well with a deep purple bellflower *Campanula glomerata*, but found it didn't.

Then I noticed a soft pale yellow marguerite (probably *Anthemis tinctoria* 'Moonlight') on the other side of the bellflower that worked perfectly as a companion. With the same misplaced confidence, I had also planted a tall, flat-topped yarrow *Achillea filipendulina* 'Coronation Gold' to face down a delphinium, the purple 'King Arthur'. Wrong again, evidently. Interestingly enough, a shorter, paler yellow achillea 'Moonshine' nearby looked just right.

I began to hunt for more plants in that same pale sulfur yellow. It wasn't until some years later that I came across the best of all soft yellows—a fluffy meadow rue, *Thalictrum speciosissimum (glaucum)*, that looks like a mop dusted with pale yellow pollen. Purple Canterbury bells (*Campanula medium*, a biennial) look wonderful against this meadow rue.

Now all this was very exciting; evidently, I reasoned, all yellows are not created equal. The whole matter of color became totally absorbing. There are many thorough and scientific studies of color, and I commend them to you, but their chief value to me was the affirmation of what I had concluded from observation. Once I found that what I judged to be successful in my garden was according to standard color theory, I relaxed and went back to moving my plants around for the pure pleasure of creating garden pictures.

As a beginning gardener I wondered why, if artists could buy their pigment by precise names, gardeners should have to settle for such rudimentary color definitions in nursery catalogs. I'm more reasonable now. To be fair, perception of color is so highly subjective that I doubt the nurseries could do much better. For another thing, I think it's important to make your own discoveries, as I did. (Meanwhile, it might be as well not to order plants with flowers described as "saucy red," "sky blue," "tropical pink," or the like.) It was the yellows that got me started, but very soon I realized there was a similar problem with other colors. What about *red*? And *blue*? Even worse.

*R*ED

The first time I realized there was something wrong with red as a color tag was when some self-seeded rose mullein (*Lychnis coronaria*) bloomed in its vivid magenta color next to a scarlet Maltese cross (*L. chalcedonica*). There were no winners in this contest, only losers. Nor was it much better when I tried putting the Maltese cross near some red phlox ('Leo Schlageter' and 'Tenor'). Both were red, both could properly be called bright, but the combination didn't work. Forget *red*—call the Maltese cross *scarlet* and the phlox *crimson*. In simplest terms, scarlet is red with a touch of yellow added; crimson is red with a touch of blue. This is what makes all the difference.

Crimson flowers are pleasing with a wide range of colors, scarlet with fewer; both are fun to play with. In a border chiefly in pastel colors—that is, in blue, white, pink, gray, and soft yellow—crimson makes an interesting addition. In early summer, carmine lupins and deep bluish red peonies fill the bill. By midsummer, such plants as crimson bee balm 'Colrain Red', a deep red gaillardia called

'Burgundy', and an achillea, 'Fire King', will lend richness. In late summer, fall asters like 'Crimson Brocade' and 'Alma Potschke' bring the season to a glowing close.

I can see using a touch of something scarlet as a sort of wake-up call to the eye, but only in a very small amount. The shape of the inflorescence has considerable bearing on how much of the color you can use. For instance, a close, dense head of scarlet Maltese cross packs a real color wallop, but the small vermilion flowers of beardtongue *Penstemon barbatus* 'Prairie Fire' are less arresting, almost delicate, and can be absorbed peacefully into the border.

If you don't want to mix the two kinds of red (one day you will) but you love scarlet, then consider treating yourself to a border—or a section of a border—planted to scarlet with some gray- or silver-leaved plants to calm it down a little.

1. Hemerocallis 'Mallard'
2. Stachys 'Silver Queen'
3. Heuchera 'Palace Purple' (bronze foliage)
4. Artemisia 'Silver Mound'
5. Sedum 'Vera Jameson'
6. Perovskia (lavender "see-through" plant)
7. Aster 'Crimson Brocade'
8. Gaillardia 'Burgundy'
9. Marrubium incanum (silver horehound)
10. Knautia macedonica (maroon pincushion)
11. Penstemon 'Huskers Red' (bronze foliage)
12. Helictotrichon (oat grass)
13. Dahlia 'Arabian Nights' (tubers)
14. Artemisia 'Lambrook Silver'
15. Phlox 'Starfire'
16. Oriental Poppy 'Beauty of Livermore'
17. Crocosmia 'Lucifer' (corms)
18. Monarda 'Gardenview Scarlet'
19. Lobelia × gerardii (red foliage)
20. Antirrhinum majus (snapdragon—'Rocket' red)

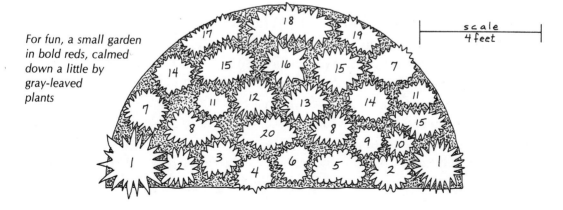

For fun, a small garden in bold reds, calmed down a little by gray-leaved plants

And magenta? Well, I still wouldn't plant *Lychnis coronaria* next to anything scarlet, but magenta can be a wonderful color if the setting is right. *Lychnis coronaria* brings its setting along with it—leaves of gray felt clasping the oddly angled stems.

I surprised myself years ago by falling in love with a geranium I saw on a visit to Sissinghurst, Vita Sackville-West's castle garden in England. It was *Geranium psilostemon*, truly magenta (not my color at all at the time), but given a gay and perky appearance by the black centers that make each flower look like a licorice candy (licorice allsorts). I further surprised myself by insisting on having it in my garden, planting it between a blue scabiosa and a big catmint. It's none too happy in Heath; the score to date is Geranium, 3; Winter, 5. But I shall keep trying. (I know—another example of what we, as sensible gardeners, shouldn't do, but every now and then there's something I want so badly that I'll grow it as an annual if I have to.) In my mind, I can see it behind the chartreuse flowers of lady's mantle.

The pinks are a special problem; in front of the word *pink* you can put about twenty qualifiers—among them, *clear, mauve, shocking, light, deep*—and still not know what color it is. Pink gets described as *lilac pink, rose pink, and lavender pink*—what color it really is depends on what particular variety of lilac, rose, or lavender the writer had in mind. This is the problem when the names we attach to colors are borrowed from other objects.

I like about as many pinks as I dislike, but I would need a painter's vocabulary of color to explain my choice. As it is, I find myself in danger of using those very terms I just decried.

Seeking help, I turned to the catalog from which I buy seed of a perfect pink snapdragon. It let me down. Normally given to excess in its descriptions of flower color, the catalog limited this one simply to *pink*.

I have used this hybrid snapdragon in many parts of the garden, where its clean, clear pink and its bold spikes contribute to pleasing combinations. Best of all these was a trio—a low *Gypsophila repens* 'Rosea' with the snapdragon seemingly coming up through it, and, behind it, a tall *Phlox paniculata* 'Fairy's Petticoat', pink with a deep rose eye. All pink, you see, but all compatible in color tone while interestingly varied in form.

Two very different pinks provide an annual treat in June—a combination of the sturdy pink pokers of *Polygonum bistorta* (knotweed) and the pale, fragile-looking *Iris sibirica* 'Fairy Dawn'. This earliest of all Siberians is in a pink that is ethereal and delicate enough to make its fanciful name acceptable.

*B*LUE

Every year there appears a roster of volunteers who are to provide flowers each Sunday in our small church. For some years it seemed that I drew the Sunday nearest to July the Fourth.

I wasn't certain, but I wondered if this was meant to be my opportunity to atone for 1776 all by myself. Anyway, I threw myself heart and soul into the red, white, and blue theme. Red was easy (I was already growing Maltese cross and *Penstemon* 'Prairie Fire'); white was no problem since 'Miss Lingard' came through every year, and there were always white irises; but *blue*!

If anchusa had survived the winter, there would be big sprays of cobalt blue flowers (I once used self-sown borage instead). Delphinium would seem to be an obvious choice, but of the tall ones in bloom many were a light Cambridge blue, or purple, or more of an opal color. The dwarf *Delphinium grandiflorum* 'Blue Mirror' would be the perfect color, but it was too early for them. Among the annuals, the dark blue love-in-a-mist (*Nigella damascena* 'Miss Jekyll') rarely bloomed that early in my garden, and the same was true of bachelor's buttons (*Centaurea cyanus*).

Some years I was lucky, but others not. I remember having to improvise with dark blue Siberian iris and light blue Jacob's ladder, but I knew very well that these were not true blues. The iris is close to purple, and Jacob's ladder is mauve.

*P*URPLE

There seems to be considerable nervousness in the trade about calling a flower purple. Real purple, the royal and regal color, belongs to *Geranium* × *magnificum*, balloon flower (though always called "blue" in catalogs), *Salvia* × *superba* 'East Friesland', clustered bellflower (*Campanula glomerata* 'Joan Elliot'), and a number of fall asters like 'Eventide' and 'Hella Lacy'. They are all in my garden because I revel in this wonderful color.

I ought to warn you that a little goes a long way, and you should certainly avoid too large a mass of any of the purples because the color can "disappear" and leave what looks like a dark hole in the border.

So many plants described as having purple flowers would be shown up as impostors if you were to put them next to the real thing. I am thinking of Kansas gayfeather (*Liatris pycnostachya*) and *Astilbe taquetii* 'Superba'.

Both of these are in a color hard to describe—definitely not purple, not pink, but what in my family we used to call (don't ask me why) an "offy" color. It's close to the heather shade often found in wool and tweeds. I notice that those who like this color refer to it approvingly as "subtle"; those who don't call it, with a sniff, "muddy."

The garden phlox 'The King', described in catalogs as purple, has been a disappointment to me because it seems much closer to magenta.

Add white to purple and you get a color with the unfashionable name of *mauve*. Worse than unfashionable, the word is almost unknown today. I'd be at a loss without it; how else could I describe the color of the summer aster (*Aster × frikartii* 'Wonder of Staffa'), the great milky bellflower (*Campanula lactiflora*), Stokes' aster (*Stokesia laevis*), the flowers of many hostas, even the humble chive flower, and a host of others?

*W*HITE

In my very early garden days, I thought white was the nervous gardener's friend; that if the compatibility of two colors was in doubt, white could be a peace-maker. How wrong! Since then, I have learned the real and extraordinary power that white has, and it's definitely not in the role of peace-maker.

What it does is to so enhance and intensify whatever color it is next to that both stand out—assail the eye, almost—and create a disturbance. When you're planting whites, remind yourself of how many different kinds of white there are or, rather, how the form of the inflorescence affects the nature of the white.

The chalkiest white I know is seen in two spring bloomers—perennial candytuft (*Iberis sempervirens*) and snow-in-summer (*Cerastium tomentosum*). I have a rose (*Rosa rugosa* 'Blanc Double de Coubert') which I bought for its heavenly perfume. It blooms off and on throughout the summer in the same astonishing white, vivid against the rugosa's typical dark green, crinkled foliage. Gertrude Jekyll called it "the whitest of all roses."

Very slightly different from chalk white is what I call laundry white; it has the shine of starched cotton. You see it in the petals of shasta daisies and in the exquisite Japanese anemone 'Honorine Jobert', with glistening white petals, the center a little bright green knob surrounded by yellow stamens.

The white I find most interesting in the border is what I think of as an antique, "weathered," or ivory white. This is the color of the white coneflower (*Echinacea purpurea* 'White Lustre'), whose sharply recurved petals make a good ruff for the rusty brown cone on top. There is a cool, greenish white in the throat of flowering tobacco (*Nicotiana alata*), and a haze of green in the cloud of false baby's breath (*Galium aristatum*).

In fact, I prefer the false to the real baby's breath (*Gypsophila paniculata* 'Bristol Fairy'), whose double flowers carry too strong a white. The species gypsophila, being single and therefore airier, is a white that inclines to gray, and is more easily absorbed into the color scheme.

Shadows at the base of crowded petals and in the throat of tubular flowers give a flush of faint color to the white. Little white flowers packed into spires, like those of bugbane (*Cimicifuga simplex*) look fluffy and faintly speckled because of the numerous prominent stamens, as do the bottlebrush flower heads of Canadian burnet (*Sanguisorba canadensis*).

I love the common name, pearly everlasting, for *Anaphalis triplinervis*, but it doesn't often look pearly to me. A day or two after opening, it merely looks grubby and on its way to brown. White flowers can age gracefully to gray, but white flowers turning brown are purely depressing, and I don't hesitate to cut them down early.

The shape and arrangement of the flower or flowers greatly affects our perception of its whiteness. I have learned to be cautious of white garden phlox, and of *Phlox maculata* 'Miss Lingard', in particular. This early phlox, called the wedding phlox because it blooms in June before the others, holds pearly white flowers on six-inch panicles. While each alone is lovely, many such heads clustered together lose delicacy, resulting in something dangerously like scoops of white pudding, very distracting in the border. Here, less is going to be more. Clumps should be held to no more than four or five stems, and neighboring plants should be in colors that do not offer too sharp a contrast.

FOLIAGE

I have gone out sometimes on a morning early in May to look at the garden. Standing at one end of the long border, looking down its length, I think I see all the greens in the world, and I wonder if that border will ever look as lovely again (this, from a gardener who wants flowers, flowers, and more flowers?). That's when I want people to see it, so they will come to know all the colors of green. ("When will it be at peak bloom?" they always ask. It's a natural question of course, if one is going to make only one visit to a garden.)

Without as yet a single flower, every plant reveals a unique identity. Strong verticals rise behind horizontal mounds. Already recognizable are the strong, the leaners, the climbers, the weavers, the ground huggers. Leaves of every size are smooth, hairy, prickly, woolly, dull, shiny. And the colors—all the way from the yellowest green to the bluest, and many of them promising change in the months to come.

Take a long look at your garden at this time of year—you're looking at what will hold the border together all season long, while the flowers come and go. Perhaps you need more than the flowering plants' own leaves; think of using some of the plants grown for their foliage alone—silver, gray, and blue.

I like to write "silver," though I know "gray" is nearer the mark. But I have seen silver, too, on a blue shrub willow after rain.

Artemisias come first to mind, from the tall, bushy 'Lambrook Silver' to the neat little 'Silver Mound'. I have tried some of the artemisias with more finely dissected foliage, but they're marginal in areas with winters colder than Zone 6 or 7, and 'Powis Castle' and 'Valerie Finnis' won't do here. I'm fairly sure it's the spring wet and the water-retentive soil that does them in more than the low winter temperatures.

I grow also *Artemisia ludoviciana* ('Silver King' and 'Silver Queen', in commerce), but with these, as with all the artemisias, it's important to keep them trimmed and, if they do manage to reach flowering stage behind your back, to cut them all the way back. White or gray turning to brown is very unattractive.

If you come across *Artemisia lactiflora* remember that this is the exception in the family. It is grown for its sprays of airy white flowers, so useful in August. The foliage is totally undistinguished, just like the common mugwort of the dunes. I rely on this artemisia's flowers to lighten up the heavier, more solid flowers of such late summer beauties as aster and helenium.

One of the grayest, woolliest, and certainly best-loved plants for foliage is lamb's ears (*Stachys byzantina*). It is so well loved by children, in fact, that in my garden the leaves that are at the edge of the border, and therefore handy, get loved half to death.

Although lamb's ears is conspicuous in borders in some of the most spectacular gardens, this plant says "cottage garden" as clearly as any. We owe a debt to those cottage gardens, humble repositories of so many plants that would otherwise have disappeared as the winds of garden fashion blew this way and that.

Lamb's ears is the plant with the obvious gray, almost white leaves for the front of the border. In humid seasons and rainy weather it can rot and look wretched, and the best thing is to pull off all the soggy leaves. Opinion is divided on the purple-pink flowers. I like to see them rising from the low mat of leaves, but if you don't want flowers, the one for you is 'Silver Carpet', a sterile cultivar.

There's no shortage of woody grays; think of lavender, santolina, and even the common sage of kitchens (*Salvia officinalis*). All three are shrublike in habit and can be cut back hard in spring, to bloom on new wood. For me, lavender is in a class by itself, an essential part of my garden (see *Cuttings,* page 82). *Santolina chamaecyparissus*, with attractive silvery gray, finely dissected leaves, offers the gardener a choice. Later in summer, this little plant covers itself with tiny yellow flowers. You may enjoy their brilliance against the gray foliage, but if bright yellow is not what you need in that part of the garden, shear them off, as I do.

Among the plants offering blue-gray foliage are some ornamental grasses. Best of all for color, in my opinion, is the blue oat grass (*Helictotrichon sempervirens*). It's beautiful in its own right, but what a foil it is for flowers of brilliant color. I cannot imagine another place in my garden for that stunning but outrageous scarlet-orange *Lychnis × arkwrightii*.

The oat grass will take a bit of space—after two years, my plants were three feet across. *Festuca glauca* is a little grass of similar color and useful in small spaces.

Rue, herb-of-grace (*Ruta graveolens*), is a beautiful plant with blue, oddly cut leaves that I wouldn't be without, although it has its dangers. After handling a number of plants on a very hot summer's day, I developed not so much a rash as a bad burn, which blistered. Too late I read a warning in an herbal: "May cause dermatitis: Wear gloves when handling."

I want to tell you about one more blue-green addition to my border, the dwarf willow (*Salix purpurea* 'Nana'). It can go to eight feet, but I cut it back each spring to keep it at about four feet and use it as a shrub at the rear of the border. (This is the plant that showed me silver.)

Unlike white, green really *is* the nervous gardener's friend, uniting and softening flower colors, but it is far more than that. Foliage, leafy and lovely, is a delight to the eye.

FILLING THE SPACE

When you look at any of the designs in this book you will see that I indicate the placement of individual plants. I do this because people following plans will often put plants in a straight line, at regular distances apart, leaving much of the allotted space empty. What I want to be sure you understand is that whether I indicate one or three or five—or whatever number of that particular plant seems right for its growth and spread—my intention is to have that space filled with a generous mass of flowers and leaves of the same kind. After the plants have settled in and are growing well, I don't care to see discrete plants, only the mass effect.

One plant, one color, should not seem to stop abruptly, as if it had hit an electric fence. In nature, plants make adventurous sallies into one another's territory, and I like the plants in my garden to do the same. I like such mingling within reason, of course—I'm not going to let some overadventurous bully like that yarrow called 'The Pearl' work its way into, through, and around a choicer neighbor. Now that might well be a case for the electric fence.

Much has been written about planting in drifts. However you care to interpret drifts, the important thing to remember is that each planting should flow into adjacent plantings. When you make the transition from plan to planting you have the opportunity to make sure this happens. The word "drift," evidently, can give rise to misunderstanding. I found a client wrestling, in some exasperation, with a large geranium she had unpotted from its two-gallon container. Hot, tired, and very cross, she plunked it down and turned to me. "I can't get the darn thing to go in drifts," she said.

I began this section by saying that it's in spring that we can truly appreciate the contribution foliage makes to the composition of a border. When the blossoms come, we see something else. Whether it rises from a fountain of leaves, like a daylily, pierces a froth of foliage, like moonbeam coreopsis, or is held under an arching leaf, like Solomon's seal, a flower owes much of its beauty to the harmony and balance of the foliage that surrounds it.

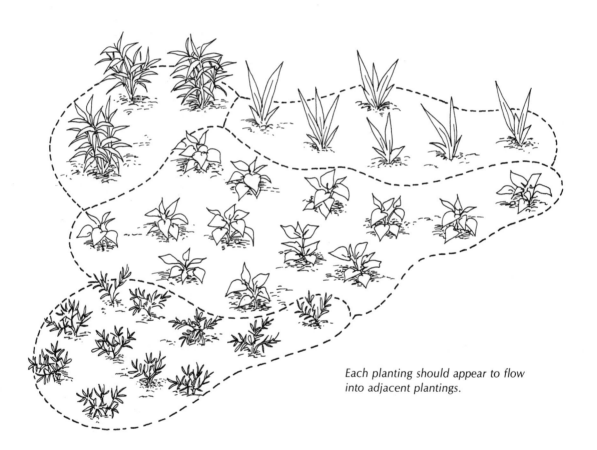

Each planting should appear to flow into adjacent plantings.

**PLANT KEY FOR PASTEL BORDER,
20′ × 5′**

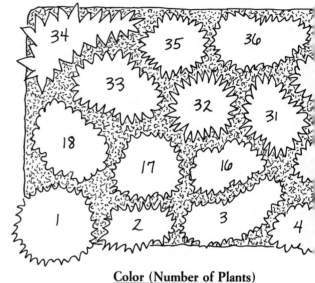

scale
5 feet

A border in pastel colors

Key	Plant	Color (Number of Plants)
1.	*Potentilla fruticosa* 'Abbotswood'	white (1)
2.	*Dianthus plumarius* 'Spring Beauty' strain	pink (3)
3.	*Perovskia atriplicifolia*	lavender (3)
4.	*Sedum* 'Vera Jameson'	purple (foliage) (1)
5.	*Delphinium grandiflorum* 'Blue Mirror'	cobalt blue (6+)
6.	*Heuchera sanguinea*	pink (3)
7.	*Artemisia schmidtiana* 'Silver Mound'	gray (1)
8.	*Geranium sanguineum lancastrense*	pink (3)
9.	*Coreopsis verticillata* 'Moonbeam'	yellow (3)
10.	*Nepeta* 'Six Hills Giant'	purple (1)
11.	*Campanula persicifolia* 'Telham Beauty'	blue (1)
12.	*Dictamnus albus* 'Purpureus'	pink (1)
13.	*Salvia* × *superba* 'East Friesland'	purple (3)
14.	*Aquilegia* × *hybrida* 'Snow Queen'	white (3)
15.	*Achillea* 'Moonshine'	yellow (3)
16.	*Dahlia* 'Park's Princess'	pink (1)
17.	*Geranium* × *magnificum*	purple (1)
18.	*Sedum purpureum* 'Autumn Joy'	pink/bronze (3)
19.	*Aster* × *frikartii* 'Wonder of Staffa'	lavender (3)
20.	*Helictotrichon sempervirens*	blue-gray (1)
21.	*Phlox maculata* 'Miss Lingard'	white (3)
22.	*Dahlia* 'Arabian Nights'	dark red (1)
23.	*Echinacea purpurea* 'Bright Star'	rose pink (1)

Key	Plant	Color (Number of Plants)
24.	*Liatris spicata*	purple (1)
25.	*Phlox paniculata* 'Tenor'	rose-red (3)
26.	*Anemone vitifolia* 'Robustissima'	pink (1)
27.	*Miscanthus sinensis* 'Silberpfeil'	green/white (1)
28.	*Delphinium* × *belladonna* 'Belladonna'	light blue (3)
29.	*Phlox paniculata* 'Bright Eyes'	pink (3)
30.	*Artemisia absinthium* 'Lambrook Silver'	gray (1)
31.	*Iris sibirica* 'Sea Shadows'	blue (3)
32.	*Paeonia lactiflora* 'Festiva Maxima'	white (1)
33.	*Phlox paniculata* 'Franz Schubert'	mauve (3)
34.	*Digitalis purpurea* 'Alba'	white (3 +)
35.	*Aster novae-angliae* 'Hella Lacy'	purple (1)
36.	*Boltonia asteroides* 'Snowbank'	white (2)
37.	*Phlox paniculata* 'Tenor'	rose red (3)
38.	*Echinops ritro* 'Taplow Blue'	steel blue (2)
39.	*Gypsophila paniculata* 'Pink Fairy'	pink (1)
40.	*Thalictrum speciosissimum*	yellow (2)
41.	*Aster novae-angliae* 'Alma Potschke'	red (1)
42.	*Sanguisorba canadensis*	white (2)
43.	*Papaver orientale* 'Helen Elizabeth'	pink (1)
44.	*Monarda didyma* 'Colrain Red'	burgundy red (1)
45.	*Baptisia australis*	blue (1)
46.	*Digitalis purpurea* 'Alba'	white (3 +)

A BORDER IN PASTEL COLORS

I know that specifics will be a lot more use to you than any number of generalizations about color, so I'd like to invite you to accompany me in the creation of a perennial border. I hope it will be the next best thing to working side by side in the garden.

I have supposed a straight, south-facing border of conventional shape, twenty feet long and five feet wide. This border could very well have a fence, a stone wall, or a hedge behind it, but I shall site it in an open area and use tall strong plants to the rear.

It is not a particularly adventurous border; I have deliberately chosen plants that are widely available and that do not pose special cultural problems. A word here about the number of plants: the total of ninety would be necessary if you hope to have the border looking filled out in its first year. Ninety good-sized plants would involve a considerable outlay right off. You can work out the approximate cost by pricing large pots of perennials at local nurseries. If this discourages you, remember, when you buy a bigger plant you're probably buying an extra year of flowers.

Five hundred dollars' worth of perennials could enrich your life for years to come. With care, five hundred dollars might buy five evenings of dinner and theater for a couple. It might. If it's not the year for either of these indulgences, you can do one of two things: you can put in a single plant where I have suggested two or three and surround it the first year with annuals—either plants or seeds, or a combination of both. Or you can buy small-sized perennials from mail-order nurseries that offer three- and six-packs of first-year plants at a low price (see *Mail-order Sources*, page 199).

Now, on to the border and its plants. There are five plants that should go in as early as possible. Four are herbaceous perennials: peony, poppy, gas plant, and baptisia; the fifth is a shrub, *Potentilla* 'Abbotswood'. Why do I think of these as important features in a perennial border? They're not particularly big, but they do have presence and they help give an established look to the planting.

It's best to order the first two of these plants from mail-order nurseries in late summer, for planting in the fall. (I am speaking here of the ideal situation; chapter one contains a schedule for the "perfect" garden.)

Recognizing that life sometimes makes it hard for us to be perfect, and that you may be making this flower bed in the spring, let me suggest that you hold places the first year for both the peony and the poppy by sowing annuals of corresponding colors. These could be annual baby's breath or hyacinth-flowered candytuft, for instance, in the spot where you will plant the white peony later, and lavatera or mallow where you plan to have the pink oriental poppy.

The peony heads the list. Its lovely clawlike crimson shoots are among the earliest risers in the garden. I choose the old-fashioned *Paeonia lactiflora* 'Festiva Maxima' here (#32) because it makes a good strong bush of handsome foliage, and because it is the archetypal peony—huge white double heads flecked with crimson in the heart of the flower, and with more fragrance than any peony I know. Yes, it may need holding up, and, yes, early wind and rainstorms may shatter it after a day or two, but don't deprive yourself of this extravagant, sensual beauty. If I had another ten feet of border, I would have put in two of them!

Long after the peony flowers are gone the plant adds dignity to the border. It also provides a background for smaller perennials, and has beautifully colored foliage in the fall. Look at the plants surrounding the peony in my plan. Behind it, a purple fall aster and a strong boltonia will flower later, but the *Iris sibirica* 'Sea Shadows' (#31) and the big purple *Geranium* × *magnificum* (#17) should be in bloom at the same time. The dahlia in front (#16) bears a multitude of pink cactus-type flowers. In my garden these bloom long enough to be seen against the lovely colors of the peony's fall foliage.

With all the talk of form and presence, what am I to say about the next one, the oriental poppy (#43)? The foliage is dark green and coarse, with much-dissected leaves. Strong stems bear huge, satin-petaled flowers that only a Georgia O'Keefe could make you believe in if you had never seen them growing. For a week or two in early summer, this poppy dominates the scene, but after the flowers are over, the foliage yellows and dies, and the plant goes dormant, leaving you looking at a big empty space. But not if you plan ahead and surround it with plants that burgeon as the poppy fades.

Look at the border design. There are big, vigorous plants behind the poppy. American burnet (*Sanguisorba canadensis*), (#42) in handsome leaf in spring, will bloom later in August, and the crimson bee balm (*Monarda didyma* 'Colrain Red') (#44) begins blooming as the poppy fades. The light blue spires of *Delphinium* 'Belladonna' (#28) rise to the left and front, and the striped grass *Miscanthus sinensis* 'Silberpfeil' (#27) to the right. The graceful green and white ribbons, moving in the slightest breeze, draw the eye. There is a dahlia of deepest red, 'Arabian Nights' (#22), planted immediately to the front; this makes heavy leaf growth and effectively fills the space left by the dear departed.

Between them, these sturdy perennials fill that part of the border so amply that you forget there had ever been a poppy there. In fact, you'll be surprised when you clear up the border at the end of the summer to discover the poppy's light green rosette of new leaves (they serve as a winter mulch).

Oriental poppies are shipped only when dormant. Order early in the summer and expect your plants to arrive any time from August on.

It surprises me that so many gardeners think of oriental poppies as flowering only in a vivid coral red. There are many splendid hybrids in glowing colors—pink, white, salmon, lavender, crimson—but this border is planned for gentle pastel colors, in the main, so my choice is a luscious pink, 'Helen Elizabeth'. Just one oriental poppy is beautiful enough to justify visiting the garden several times a day, but don't think (as a friend of mine did) that because one is glorious, half a dozen would be even better. Oriental poppies are not modest flowers, and more than one in a border this size would be overwhelming. (And another thing—just think of all those holes when they go dormant.)

The old-fashioned gas plant, *Dictamnus albus* (#12), is another perennial which, like the peony, looks more shrublike and permanent than it is. It's an herbaceous perennial with glossy leaves and strong form. If that was all it offered it would be welcome, but it has, in addition, a lemony fragrance, attractive flowers, and even more attractive and long-lasting seedpods. I have chosen *D. a.* 'Purpureus' for its dark-veined, pink-purple flowers which will provide a strong note behind the soft yellow of *Coreopsis* 'Moonbeam' (#9) and the pale pink of *Geranium sanguineum lancastrense* (#8).

To the rear of the border, I've placed another shrub look-alike. It, too, is an herbaceous perennial, false indigo (*Baptisia australis*) (#45) whose leaves and flowers are pealike. It is the indigo blue color of the long racemes of flowers that make this such a visual delight in early summer; it should be lovely against the white foxglove spires. The seedpods are attractive for a while (and noisy, too—children like to rattle them as they pass by) but in a wet season they blacken and mold. Baptisia is generous with its seed, and you're likely to find countless little plants each spring.

The last of the five plants really *is* a shrub, though it might be better to call it a "shrublet," as a garden friend of mine so engagingly dubs it. This shrubby cinquefoil, *Potentilla fruticosa* 'Abbottswood' (#1), should be cut back severely each spring, after which it blooms prolifically, covering the stems with small white flowers like nickel-sized roses.

I have chosen the potentilla for the left front of the border to take the curse off the 90-degree corner. Careful clipping early in the year can encourage a pleasing, rounded shape which effectively "turns the corner." (If you like matched symmetry more than I do, you could put another 'Abbottswood' at the right front corner, or switch to the big catmint (#10) for both corners.) The value of these plants lies in their ability to "anchor" the border at each end without being so dense and lumpy as to overpower the other perennials.

Working from the corners in toward the center will make it easier to keep your bearings while you are planting. Look at the two rear corners; they provide the only example of a matched pair. I think they're needed here, and they should be plants with flowers in spires, such as white foxgloves, *Digitalis purpurea* 'Alba' (#34 and #46). If the border has anything in the way of a dark background, or if there are evergreens or woods even at some distance away, the white will be successful. But if you have neither, you should consider growing 'Excelsior Hybrids' in shades of pink and deep rose.

Most beautiful of all would be *Digitalis × mertonensis*, a hybrid foxglove in a rich pink color. Sad to say, I have to go and admire this beauty in other people's gardens; my Zone 5 winters and wet springs have killed it in each of the five years I've tried it. I have suggested a minimum of three plants in each corner, but five would allow you to extend them around the inside of the corners like sheltering arms. After the foxglove's main spire of flowers is past, there will be lateral spikes blooming lower down, and, later still, rosettes of leaves that persist over winter, serving as the plant's mulch.

There are plants for each corner that will take over when the foxglove color is gone. Look at the rear left corner on the plan. The mauve phlox, 'Franz Schubert', and the purple aster (#33 and #35) offer late summer flowers on big plants. They will reach their height (about three and a half feet and five feet, respectively) after the foxgloves fade.

At about the same time, in the right rear corner, the pink Japanese anemone, *Anemone vitifolia* 'Robustissima', will be holding up its candelabra of silvery pink flowers above dark green, grapelike leaves. I have found this anemone slow to take hold at first but it is described by some as invasive. (I would like it to invade this corner.) I remember it in England as a strong colonizer, but it's only a modest spreader for me. It's a very late riser in spring, so be careful when you're cultivating; new shoots often appear a foot or more away from the main clump.

If you find it difficult to make the transition from plan to planting, you can make it easier for yourself by planting the fluffy yellow meadow rue first, *Thalictrum speciosissimum* (#40), because it happens to be exactly in the middle of the back of the border.

Are you nervous about a yellow plant in this border of pinks, blues, grays, purples, and soft reds? Don't be. Meadow rue is not an assertive color; it is a sulfur yellow, made to appear even softer because of the pollen-dusted look of the fluffy flower head. In fact, it is exactly what is needed to counteract the "baby boutique" effect of all the pinks and blues of this time of the year. Meadow rue does not repeat bloom, but the foliage is delightful all season long, a delicate blue-green reminiscent of columbine leaves.

If I were not trying to keep this design simple by limiting the range of plants, I'd put a few tall bearded iris, perhaps 'Heavenly Blue', around the meadow rue, whose soft foliage could conceal the iris leaves when they begin to look tatty, as they do soon after blooming.

I have described already my early discoveries about the color yellow, and now, in this border, you can see how the soft ones work. *Coreopsis verticillata* 'Moonbeam' (#9) is gentle enough to be a good companion for the pale pink hardy geranium (#8) at the front edge. At the same time it works well in both color and form with the big catmint, *Nepeta* 'Six Hills Giant' (#10), on the other side of it.

The third touch of soft yellow is provided by a yarrow, *Achillea* 'Moonshine' (#15). Take a look at the plants surrounding it—delicate in form, for the most part, and every one of their colors compatible—white columbine, cobalt blue low delphinium, a bronzed purple sedum, and mauve *Aster × frikartii*. Later in the summer, the Russian sage, *Perovskia atriplicifolia* (#3), will dip its lavender wands over the flat-topped 'Moonshine' for another pleasing picture.

Going down the list of plants in this border, I am unable to find a single one that would not be happy with any of these soft yellows. The only impossible partner would be a bright yellow.

I have always loved the early white phlox, *Phlox maculata* 'Miss Lingard' (#21), but I've learned to use it with discretion. In this design, it faces down a trio of light blue delphiniums (#28), and although bright, it is acceptable for early summer, when simple, uncomplicated color schemes seem so right. There should not, however, be such bright contrast with other neighbors. Most of them are safe with white—the blue-green oat grass (#20), soft pink coralbells (#6), and a tuft of 'Silver Mound' (#7), but I fear 'Miss Lingard's' relationship to the dark red dahlia, 'Arabian Nights' (#22), may turn out to be too stark, in which case I might reduce the number of white flower heads.

There are seven whites in this border and no two are alike. The earliest to bloom are the foxgloves, whose white is often tempered by spots or freckles inside the tubular flowers. The complex flowers of the aquilegia (#14), with the slight difference in color of petals and sepals and the airy movement of the spurs, do not seem too solidly white. The shrub, potentilla 'Abbottswood', has silvery green leaves like a strawberry's and the bush appears studded with small white buttercup flowers relieved by prominent yellow stamens. The fully double peony, 'Festiva Maxima', has its whiteness broken up by flecks of crimson.

Two late-blooming whites have inflorescences so individual that they could be grown next to each other and still offer variety. *Sanguisorba canadensis* (#42) has cylindrical spikes of tiny white flowers with stamens prominent enough to break up the white. Still later in the summer comes *Boltonia asteroides* 'Snowbank' (#36). It imitates a tall aster, presenting small spiky white daisies on slender multibranched stems. The effect is not in the least like a snowbank; it's more a constellation of tiny stars.

Finally, there's my favorite phlox, the early white 'Miss Lingard', which, as I have mentioned before, turned out to be the most difficult white to handle. As a general rule, I like a bold mass of phlox, and I do not thin out the stems to the recommended three or four. But that's for all the other phlox colors. Something about the arrangement of flowers on 'Miss Lingard' results in an overall blob of white, a blancmange almost, so distracting to the eye that it is hard to focus on the rest of the border. So I cut about half the flower heads for the house, leaving space between the remaining heads. (Is this eating your cake and having it, too?)

And do not forget as you plan and consider your planting: space in the garden is more than the absence of plants; it is an element in design.

CHAPTER 10

. . . .

THE GARDEN
IN LATE SUMMER

I can't count the number of times people tell me that they like perennials, and then go on to say, "They certainly make a great show in early summer, but of course it's all over by July." They're thinking of that wonderful (I almost said outrageous) display put on in June when everything seems to happen at once, with irises, oriental poppies, and peonies all exploding into color. Well, it's true; if the Big Three of early summer were all they had in their gardens, then it would largely be plain old green for the rest of the season.

I want to show you that a perennial flower garden can unfold month by lovely month through the summer and still delight you with its offerings in fall. I'm not saying that the late summer garden is going to be a riot of color (I once heard a lecturer say that he was not in favor of riots anywhere, least of all in his garden). The color will not rival the main summer show (you could drown in color in June and July), nor should it. The late summer garden is another country; it has a quiet, gentle, almost contemplative quality.

The flowers that have bloomed all summer can begin to look a little tired, and the whole garden could use an infusion of fresh forms and colors. This takes a bit of planning, but I have my sights set on September and beyond. For the color and interest I want in my garden at that time of year, I have to consider three groups of perennials:

- Late by design: Plants that are not expected to bloom, and do not bloom, until late August, September, and—in a few cases—October
- Second chances: Perennials that bloom earlier in the summer and that will,

if cut down in time, respond with a completely new flush of both foliage and flowers.

- The workhorses: Garden stalwarts that just keep on keeping on throughout the season. Most need a little help from their friends, however, and that's going to be you.

*L*ATE BY DESIGN

The first of these groups is the easiest; the plants are all out there, in mail-order and local nurseries. All it takes is some advance study of perennials and their blooming times, judicious and timely mail-ordering (I know it's hard to think September when you're writing orders in January, but do it anyway), and visits to local nurseries at regular intervals to see what's available.

So many garden enthusiasts rush round to the local nurseries on that First Day of Spring and assume that after that the nurseries disappear until the First Day of Spring of the next year. Wrong! They're putting out plants, week by week, right through the season. And remember, when the last pack of marigolds has been sold, they have a lot more time to answer your questions about perennials.

In my September garden, the plants designed to bloom late provide some of the strongest elements, for many of them are relatively large, and some have commanding and dramatic presence. Something else they bring to the late garden is a freshness and a newness that enliven a scene that has by now become familiar. This is what creates the excitement in a perennial flower garden, the sense that there is always more to come and that every day will bring change.

If you couldn't name any other flowers that typify autumn in the garden, I'm sure you could come up with "aster." As a child, I knew these in England (where I would have liked them better if they hadn't signaled the beginning of the school year). We called all of them Michaelmas daisies (pronounced mickle-muss), for they were the flowers that bloomed at the time of St. Michael's Mass, the end of the third quarter of the year. In this country, they are listed as New England asters (*Aster novae-angliae*) and New York asters (*A. novi-belgi*).

Asters are marvelous flowers because no one of their rich and glowing colors is incompatible with another. I think of them as stained-glass colors, an association with harvest festivals in the local church, where they were massed against the altar rail.

In size, these asters range from twelve-inch dwarfs to towering five- and six-footers. Back in fashion now, and recognized for the beauties they are, they were at one time thought of as commonplace and undesirable. Well, beauty lies in the eye of the beholder, and the beholders of that time were dazzled by the novelty of the newly imported exotics of the Victorian era. Unappreciated in their native land, these North American asters were snatched up by British plant hunters, who took them back to England and hybridized them.

I have three particularly good performers in my garden. *Aster novae-angliae* 'Alma Potschke', has a glowing rose-red flower, blooming from August to the end of September. *Aster novi-belgi* 'Eventide', is a September bloomer of deep purple with a yellow center. *Aster novae-angliae* 'Harrington's Pink', the tallest and latest of all, is a magnet for butterflies and bees well into October.

Japanese anemone pairs well with asters. One of the hardier ones, *Anemone vitifolia* 'Robustissima', holds its silvery pink flowers in an airy candelabrum that shows to advantage against the denser flowers and leaves of the aster 'Eventide'. Just because I'm anxious to have late color doesn't mean I want to put up with miserable-looking foliage all summer, so I really appreciate the handsome grapelike leaves of these anemones. They take their time appearing in spring, and they're a bit wayward about where they emerge, but whenever and wherever they do, they're always welcome in my garden.

The most elegant of all the Japanese anemones is a pure white that rejoices in the lovely name of 'Honorine Jobert'. It's a little harder to bring through severe winters and will sometimes bloom so late that an early frost nips the petals and turns them brown. But what other flowers have this delicacy and sheen to them, and where else can you find such glistening white and such silvered pink at this late date? I marvel when I pass them, and I'm grateful.

There are some thrilling dark blues in the September garden. One of them, with hooded, almost sinister, flowers (and which is, in fact, extremely poisonous in all its parts), is *Aconitum carmichaelii*, the purplish blue monkshood. The flowers are so dark that they photograph poorly; as an ideal companion offering a background that shows it up, I have the tall aster 'Harrington's Pink', with the Japanese anemone 'Honorine Jobert' beside it.

A lovely deep "true" blue is provided by *Salvia grandiflora pitcheri*. The tubular, lipped flowers are borne on two- to three-foot stems, which either flop about aimlessly or collapse on the ground. I can't bear to see such wands staked, so I plant this salvia close to, almost on top of, a Japanese anemone and draw the long stems up through the anemone foliage. The silvery pink and rich blue make a lovely combination.

I've noticed visitors stop and stare, then finger one of the blue flowers and try to trace it down to see where it comes from. The basal foliage is wretched, and, in my opinion, just as well hidden. In my own defense, I must say that it doesn't seem to suffer from being smothered down there among the leaves of more robust plants.

Salvia is a big genus. From the southern and western United States and Mexico come many salvias that are wonderful in fall. I know, because I've seen them in gardens in Zone 6 and southward. Not in mine, alas.

There's nothing like purple for richness in the late garden. The native joe-pye weed (*Eupatorium purpureum*) is a common sight in the wild, and there is now a German cultivar named 'Gateway' that is part of a favorite trio in my garden. 'Gateway' has purple flower heads, but even more attractive are its purple stems. Next to this is a six-foot *Angelica gigas*, a most dramatic plant with huge alliumlike domes of purple, starry flowers and, again, purple stems. To the front of these is a white baneberry (*Actaea pachypoda*), a native you've probably seen on walks in the woods. For much of the year it's not an eye-catcher, but in fall—with clusters of dead-white berries and a purple-black dot at the tip of each—it justifies its popular name, doll's-eyes.

Grown in the half shade against a birch wood, what a trio these plants make! As if the color were not enough, in a certain light their purple stems almost disappear and the flowers seem to float, lending an air of mystery to the autumn scene.

There are two late-blooming plants whose bright color might be welcome among these somber purples. *Physostegia* 'Vivid' is a cultivar of the familiar native, obedient plant, or false dragonhead, but 'Vivid' blooms considerably later, in a vibrant rose pink, so aptly described in its name. *Chelone obliqua*, the most ornamental of the turtleheads, offers bright rose purple flowers. Both plants do well in moderate shade, though they can take full sun as long as there is sufficient moisture.

If there is one color that is abundant (some might say relentless) at the end of summer, it is yellow. A lot of this color comes from flowers that are so much a part of this time of year that they are either taken for granted and barely noticed, or scorned and dismissed as boring. Perhaps it is true that familiarity breeds contempt.

In the past, I was not very charitable in my opinion of goldenrod, or the ubiquitous 'Golden Glow'. I think there's a good reason for that. I associated goldenrod with the bedraggled plants I used to see growing on London bomb sites during World War II—it was not a cheery sight. Similarly, 'Golden Glow', neither golden nor glowing, but barely surviving in sour soil at the foot of some area steps, did nothing to lift my spirits. But both of them look wonderful in the clearer, sunnier North American autumn. Why not? This is their own, their native land.

When I first came across 'Golden Glow', I didn't recognize it. I was out looking for flowers to brighten the dim interior of an old barn that was to be the scene of a wedding party. With one day to go to the wedding and panic setting in, I was driving along a back road, when against an old shed I saw this wonder, a huge bush of brilliant yellow flowers. When I went to the nearby farmhouse and asked the owner if I could have some, she was more than generous. "What, that old yellow daisy?" she said, "have it all, before it takes the shed down with it."

I filled a milk churn, barrels, and even old sap buckets with these golden flowers, and the interior of the barn came to life. Clipping some of the flowers to six-inch stems, I filled enough jelly jars for the length of all the trestle tables. 'Golden Glow' had to be our candles, for a naked flame was out of the question in that dry barn.

Hybridizers have been at work on both these golden beauties (you see, I'm quite converted), developing plants of more manageable size, better suited to today's gardens. I have a most becoming little goldenrod in my garden, *Solidago* 'Golden Fleece'. It grows to a mound no more than two feet tall and two feet across with compact, bright yellow flowers, attractive broad leaves, and none of the legginess associated with the taller, old goldenrods.

I looked up 'Golden Glow', and found it under *Rudbeckia laciniata* 'Hortensia', where it was described as invasive and largely replaced in gardens by the superior *Rudbeckia nitida* 'Goldquelle'. Of course! That must be the plant I've enjoyed every September for years. It's growing next to an amethyst sea holly whose prickly, metallic flower heads show to great advantage against 'Goldquelle's' shaggy yellow heads.

I'm sure there are countless gardens in late summer full of sunflowers, sneezeweed, tickseed, gloriosa daisies, golden marguerites, and bright yellow chrysanthemums. It must be a jolly sight, but I can well believe it might pall after a year or two. It's not just that so many of the late summer flowers are yellow, but that they tend to be daisies or daisy look-alikes. Most are fibrous-rooted, fast-growing, and large at maturity, and the yellow they sport is frequently assertive.

I hang around nurseries and garden centers quite a bit, and I'm fascinated by some of the things I hear. A common question in late summer is: "Do you have anything that's not a yellow daisy?" Well, of course they do, and plenty of them.

We've already considered some purples and blues. If you like bold combinations, just imagine what a purple aster such as 'Eventide' or the dark blue monkshood could do for gloriosa daisies or any of the family of black-eyed Susans.

If these combinations are a little too much for you, you can turn with relief to the interesting whites of late summer. There is one plant I have grown for many years and which I now regard as the unsung hero of the late garden. It comes through drought, wet, and wind.

Let me introduce you to *Boltonia asteroides* 'Snowbank', a cultivar of a plant native to the eastern and central United States. 'Snowbank' grows into a bush from three to five feet tall, studded with small daisylike flowers in fall. I'm a fan of this plant, as you can tell. In the first place, its gray-green leaves are a gentle presence in the border all summer long; and second, it never needs staking.

'Snowbank' is so strong, indeed, that it often serves to hold up the weaker brethren. I've seen it after a storm standing like a rock, with plants fallen into it from all sides. There is a pink form, too, *Boltonia* 'Pink Beauty', recently made available; it is lovely, blooming a little earlier than 'Snowbank', but don't look to it for strength, because it is a lax grower and needs support.

Spires of flowers can give a lift to any border, and white spires are particularly dramatic in fall. Snakeroot, or bugbane (*Cimicifuga racemosa*), is a native that blooms in early to midsummer, but for really late bloom, *Cimicifuga simplex* 'The Pearl' is the snakeroot to have. Blooming in October, 'The Pearl', like the white Japanese anemone, runs the risk of damage from early frost, but it's so lovely that I'm prepared to take that risk. It has given me glistening, bottlebrush flowers for five years out of seven, and in the other two, I simply cut off the frosted brown spikes and enjoyed the foliage.

For more white, there's *Artemisia lactiflora* that begins to bloom in August. This one is not what we expect of artemisias. It is grown for its flowers and has undistinguished dark green leaves. The airy sprays of greenish white flowers at a height of four to five feet are attractive toward the back of the border and contrast effectively with more substantial flower forms such as asters and heleniums.

So much for the tall whites, but there are whites for the front of the border, too. I count on garlic chives (*Allium tuberosum*) for a refreshing white in August. The leaves are straplike, in a bright green that's pleasing all through the summer. The flowers are scintillating balls of white, but before that there are the buds, and what buds! I think the beauty of some buds exceeds anything the open flowers have to offer.

These slim, sharply pointed, tightly wrapped promises are just translucent enough to suggest how intricately the florets must be folded and crumpled inside. The buds don't all open at once, so there will be both buds and flowers on the plant at the same time. After more than a month of flowers, the seed heads on their strong stems remain a handsome feature in the border, though some gardeners dread the proliferation of seedlings.

For the front edge of the flower bed there is a low-growing white daisy (*Chyrsanthemum weyrichii*), whose thick lustrous leaves almost qualify it as a ground cover. It must be grown in full sun to flower. Don't make the mistake I did with this latest of all fall bloomers. It was in sun when I planted it in May but by late August it was in shade most of the day, and of course needed another six weeks of sun to bring on the flowers. Once moved to a spot that guaranteed sun, it bloomed in mid-October for two years out of three. I admit this is stretching late-season blooms to the limit, but I love to see those white daisies, some of them fading to pink, among the brilliant fallen leaves.

Seeing what an ornament the wild clematis was, clambering over bushes and through the grass around the pond, I planted a sweet autumn clematis (*Clematis paniculata*) to cover some old posts in the garden. It certainly did what it was supposed to; every year for years it covered itself with sweet-smelling, starry flowers in October. Later its name was changed by edict, so I did The Right Thing. After all, I told myself, I have students in the garden every summer and I have to show them I know what's what. So I pulled out the by-now almost illegible old label and put in a spanking new one. "*Clematis maximowicziana*," it said. That winter, the poor thing died. Too much for it, I suppose. Grow it without a label; you'll love it.

I count the pond's edge planted with white iris as part of my garden, but there is a wildness there that can surprise and delight me. One September, wild clematis with quaint names—virgin's bower, traveler's joy, old man's beard—trailed out from the surrounding woodland to the edge of the pond. Magically, the deep blue flowers of bottle gentian appeared at the same time. There they were—a colony of *Gentiana andrewsii*, little blue bottles in a sea of clematis stars, the water giving the picture back in reflection. Now there was a pure gift—no strings attached. But I could take inspiration from it, and I did. I planted a late monkshood of the same mysterious blue at the base of my autumn clematis.

I'm writing about gentians and monkshood here, in a section on white flowers, because I cannot think of any flower in isolation; I visualize each as part of a small garden scene and, if one is a newcomer to my garden, in a scene I must create. This is where my happiness in gardening lies.

SECOND CHANCES

Right up there with the big showstoppers of early summer, there are beautiful perennials that are almost as spectacular, fully as lovely, and that have, in addition, the potential to bloom again later in the year.

Take the most spectacular of all, often called the queen of the June border—delphinium. Garden parties are planned to coincide with its flowering (unfortunately, so are early summer rainstorms). For two or three weeks delphinium crowns the border and when the flowers fade it seems unlikely that after such a splendid show the plant could do anything but rest until another year.

But have faith. Cut down the flower stalks, keeping an eye on the foliage below. It is losing much of its vigor and beginning to look dull and tired, but move the old leaves aside and you will see fresh bright leaf buds rising from the crown. This is the point at which I remove the old leaves, cultivate around the plant, and then water, adding liquid fertilizer.

What this plant then does in my garden seems a miracle to me. It throws up a mound of new leaves as if spring were starting all over again, and after a few weeks follows it up with another flowering. This time the stems are shorter than before, but I can't complain. To have those colors back in August and September is a blessing.

Although many perennials can be encouraged to bloom again, relatively few

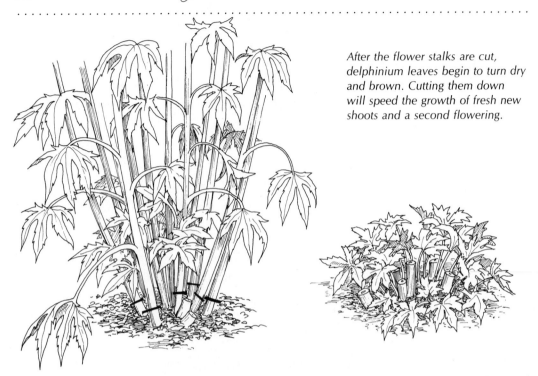

After the flower stalks are cut, delphinium leaves begin to turn dry and brown. Cutting them down will speed the growth of fresh new shoots and a second flowering.

will respond as the delphinium does, by throwing up a completely new flush of foliage as well as flowers, but globe thistle (*Echinops ritro*) is one. If you cut off the flower heads as they mature and turn dusty gray, you will be rewarded by fresh steel-blue flowers, which are far more attractive anyway.

Soon the supply of flowers will come to an end and the foliage, like that of delphinium, will lose vigor and begin to turn brown. Cut off the old leaves and reveal the bright new leaves bursting from the crown. Water, feed, and stand back, for here comes a brand new plant—leaves, flowers and all, only a little shorter than the earlier one, and most welcome in late summer.

Shasta daisy, perennial cornflower, yarrow, and false hollyhock (*Sidalcea*) are among others that can be cut back severely to encourage new leaves and flowers.

A small plant that needs this treatment but that poses a special problem is 'Silver Mound' (*Artemisia schmidtiana*). Being an artemisia, it's grown for its tight little mound of foliage, and not for its flowers. Just about the time that the unattractive mustard-colored flowers appear, the stems splay out from the center and the delightful mound shape is lost. It should be cut down at this stage or, better still, just before this stage. It then begins a fresh burst of silver-gray leaves and it will be a true silver mound again in a few weeks.

But there is an awkward hiatus. Whereas the bigger plants further back in the border are decently concealed by neighboring plants while they're making their second growth, 'Silver Mound', at a height usually under twelve inches, is at the very front of the border. I grow my plants so close together that I can usually persuade a neighboring plant to lean over the cut-down 'Silver Mound' until it begins to grow back. Once it was a blue flax that obliged in this way; another time, a small catmint. Actually, "persuade" is not quite the right word; what I do is to nudge the neighboring plant over a little and push in twigs to hold it, and then draw some flowering stems over the top of the temporarily bald 'Silver Mound'.

At first, when I was nervous about the possible effects of my ministrations, I cut down the back half of the plant and fluffed up the front to hide it. When the new growth was a few inches high, I cut the front.

I have students who still can't bear to do the whole operation in one fell swoop. I can't blame them. As a matter of fact, it's not a bad way to approach any drastic job on a plant you don't yet know well. Try out your technique on the back of the plant, and watch what happens. New gardeners may feel better or, at least, not so bad about cutting down a plant if they understand that those old leaves are no longer useful to it. The plant has finished with them; their work has now been taken over by the young foliage.

When these cutback plants come into their second round of foliage and bloom they tend to be shorter than they were first time around. This is something I take into account when planning the sequence of bloom in the border. I find it provides me with a good opportunity to make new and interesting color combinations partway through the season. The globe thistle that paired well with the tall ligularia 'The Rocket' in late June and early July becomes a partner for a pink coneflower in August and September, when the ligularia is nothing more than brown seed heads on dry stalks. Delphinium that rose above the peonies and poppies of June is now of a height to associate easily with the second bloom of *Achillea* 'Moonshine'. It's an endlessly fascinating game, with as many plays as there are gardeners.

THE WORKHORSES

There is a third group of perennials that provide late summer color. These are the workhorses of the garden, many of which have sustained the borders with their color since early summer, either steadily or sporadically. I'm thinking of such stalwarts as coneflower, blanketflower, salvia, veronica, summer aster, campanula. If you don't want these plants to look like leftovers by the end of August, you must take care of them throughout the season.

Deadheading is of prime importance. I don't like to use the word "chore" for any garden work, but that's what this is, a chore. By preventing the formation of seed, you will greatly improve the quantity and quality of flowers to come, to say nothing of smartening up the plant. Don't think of it as merely deadheading, or "pulling the heads off flowers."

If you approach the job thoughtfully, you'll see that it's almost like pruning. By careful cutting in the right places, you can encourage the plant to branch, thus improving its whole shape, just as you would a shrub or tree. These are only herbaceous perennials, of course, but why not have them looking as beautiful as possible.

Next in order of importance come all the rest of those jobs involved in keeping a flower garden growing and looking good. I lump them together for a reason. In my closely planted borders, a certain amount of maneuvering is needed to get into the middle. Once in, I'd better take advantage of the opportunity to do a thorough check. From this vantage point, I see things that were not visible from the edge of the border.

Bending down to lift a stem and support it with a twig or stake, I see a few weeds. They're small, but I pull them anyway, except for one, a dandelion. No use breaking it off at the soil level; that long-taprooted thing calls for a deep weeder. I get the feeling that this patch of garden is very dry, so I dig down an inch or so to check for moisture. I squash a Japanese beetle. Come to think of it, doesn't this part of the garden look a bit "off"? Nothing actually dying or diseased or anything as drastic as that, just not vigorous and fresh-looking. I respond to that by aerating the soil carefully between the plants. I could use a hand fork but I rely on a scuffle hoe, a wonderful tool, and my favorite (see *Tools, page 99*).

Now all this could involve four or five trips to fetch tools and supplies, plus four or five scrambles in and out of the border. I know, because that's how I worked at first (it's sadly true that "we get too soon old and too late smart," but I do like to think there's been some improvement).

So here's the lesson of this: get your tools and other supplies together first,

and while you're about it see that the hose is connected and handy, so you can water afterward as needed. Take them into the border with you and set them down as close as possible to where you're going to make a start, so you can just reach your hand out and get what you need. I say the minimum equipment you should have handy is: hand fork, deep weeder, scuffle hoe, twigs and stakes, twine, clippers, and a bucket or basket for weeds and clippings.

If I were handing out prizes, I'd have to begin with summer aster (*Aster × frikartii*), quite different from the New England asters of fall. This one begins to bloom in June and goes on right through the season until cut down by severe frost in October. For all the toughness that its performance suggests, *A. × frikartii* is almost delicate in appearance, growing in a gentle, shapely mound, covered with yellow-centered lavender daisies. Why the prize? Each flower, as it dies, shrivels and disappears beneath the foliage—no deadheading. First prize!

Catmint is another plant that requires a minimum of attention. I find that in the borders of my wide open garden, the big catmint (*Nepeta* 'Six Hills Giant')

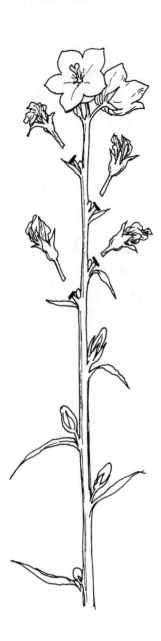

*Peach bells
(Campanula persicifolia)
need deadheading to be
their best, but are a
challenge and a trial.*

looks best. It blooms right up to frost and beyond. I have a choice; I can shear it for new
bloom on a more compact plant, or leave it as an
informal, billowing, mound. Either way, it still
sends up flowers. What I do depends on where
it's growing and on its relationship to neighboring plants, which changes from year to year.

Blanketflower (*Gaillardia aristata*) and purple
coneflower (*Echinacea purpurea*) are two plants
that look better tidied up, but that will continue
blooming even without this housekeeping. I like
to leave a few seed heads on some of the tallest
stems.

I would put *Salvia* × *superba* 'East Friesland'
among the top ten performers for both color and
long period of bloom. Purple flower spikes rise
above clumps of grayish green foliage. Like those
of many of the salvias, the flowers are surrounded
by bracts, these of a reddish purple. So lovely are
their colors and shapes that I usually leave them
for several weeks, cutting them back only when
the rich color has completely faded. They bloom
anew later in the season.

Spike speedwell (*Veronica spicata*) makes my
list, too, either in white ('Icicle') or in a rich rose
('Red Fox'). Both are long-blooming. Sheared in
midsummer, they will send up new flowers, a
few at a time. A smaller veronica (*V. incana*) has
flowers in pink or purple, but they are not the
reason for growing the plant, which is valued
more for its silver-gray leaves. I take shears to
these when they begin to look tatty, and they
quickly grow back.

I've saved two of my list of stalwarts until last
because they're such a nuisance; but they are

lovely things and I can't seem to do without them. I like all campanulas; unfortunately, the one I like best is an alarming seeder and—as if this weren't enough—a perfect misery to deadhead. Peach bells (*Campanula persicifolia*), in blue or white, first bloom in June but can be kept in flower after that by scrupulous deadheading. The job calls for nail scissors (cuticle scissors, even) with blades sharp-pointed and narrow enough to cut off one faded bell at a time without getting the bud that's alongside it. As I write this, I've decided it must go, but I think I say this every year.

Threadleaf tickseed (*Coreopsis verticillata*) is a deadheading problem too. The best, 'Moonbeam', is covered with pale yellow daisies by the hundred. 'Zagreb', has bright yellow daisies in similar numbers. Three-foot 'Grandiflora', has the brightest flowers of all. None is possible to deadhead, or so I find, and the presence of brown and withered flowers among the yellow is most unattractive.

The redoubtable Fred McGourty may have the solution. Pushed for an answer to the question of how to deal with this, he suggested shearing it right back and leaving on vacation for two or three weeks. I may have to try that.

I see that nowhere in these three groups of color providers have I mentioned phlox or daylilies, and both play a big role in my garden. There isn't a lot to say here about hemerocallis because, except for the removal of spent flowers every day, they come very close to being no-maintenance plants.

What I do want to say is that it's worth taking the trouble to seek out cultivars that bloom late in the year. I notice that it comes as a surprise to visitors to see daylilies heavily budded in September. I have three beautiful multibranched, small-flowered October bloomers—a rose red, an apricot, and a near-orange. Obviously, at this point I ought to reel off their names, but I can't: I bought them when they caught my eye at a nursery field many Septembers ago.

If you go to a daylily farm to buy plants, it will probably be some time in July, because that's when there's the most to see. Buy some, by all means, but don't blow your whole daylily budget. Poke around and find the rows where the plants are just showing bud. Go back later, when they're fully open, and make another selection. These will be the backbone of your late-summer and early-fall garden. If you're buying daylilies by mail, read the fine print in the catalog and order some marked "L" (for late). Last piece of advice: label carefully or mark the varieties on your garden plan, so that you can do better than I do when admirers ask for their names.

A RAINBOW OF PHLOX, JULY TO SEPTEMBER

Here is a collection of *Phlox paniculata* cultivars, listed in their usual order of bloom in my garden (their height is between two and a half and four feet, and varies with the season and soil quality):

- 'Tenor': Deep rose; longest-blooming of all here; good in most combinations.
- 'Leo Schlageter': Rich red, toward crimson.
- 'Starfire': Brilliant red, toward scarlet; good dark foliage.
- 'White Admiral': Well-branched flower heads; good midseason white.
- 'Bright Eyes': A crimson eye and light pink petals make it seem to wink at you.
- 'The King': Described as "rich purple," but the color inclines toward magenta.
- 'Dresden China': Delicate pink flowers of outstanding size on huge trusses.
- 'Franz Schubert': Pale lavender flowers with suggestion of a white edge.
- 'Eva Cullum': Pink with a red eye; a sturdy grower and good multiplier.
- 'World Peace': Tall plant; large flowers of purest white; late summer into fall.

The outstanding white 'Miss Lingard' is not listed here; it belongs under *Phlox maculata*, and blooms two or three weeks earlier.

For me, a garden could not be a summer garden without summer phlox. *Phlox paniculata* is a glory. Even these words on the page waft the scent toward me and give me visions of their color. For me, phlox is wrapped in associations which are hard to pin down—to think of where, of when, but overwhelming nevertheless. A garden in Gloucestershire? My grandfather's? A four-year-old in a party dress (with wings, no less) lifted up and set down to smile for a snapshot beside a mass of phlox, the flowers at eye level and higher, and butterflies, everywhere. But there is no such snapshot. In my inherited collection of faded sepia prints, the nearest to that enchanted memory is a snapshot of me standing stiffly, in party regalia again (but, significantly, no wings this time), in the wrong garden, holding a stiff bunch of white daisies, and looking sullen. Of this garden, though it is documented on film, I have no recollection.

The phlox season in my garden begins with *Phlox maculata* 'Miss Lingard' (formerly *P. carolina*), often called the wedding phlox (blooms in June, obviously). A week or two later, the traditional garden phlox, *P. paniculata* begins in earnest, and continues to bloom, sporadically, until the very last one of them all blooms in October.

I grow fourteen named phlox hybrids, in white, pink, salmon, red, orange, purple, and mauve. All are beautiful, all are sweetly scented, and each has its own subtle coloration. Lecture audiences enjoy seeing slides of phlox in beautiful color combinations, but their questions reveal considerable nervousness and anxiety. Their thoughts seem mainly on disease and disaster.

To questions of what I do about powdery mildew and how I deal with red spider mites, I can only answer: nothing. Lame, I know, but I must be honest. Mildew is nonexistent some years, slight in others, and, just once, it was truly awful. Some years, it would mar one phlox; other years another; but only once did it turn all of them, pristine 'Miss Lingard' included, into ugly sticks. My remedy that year was to cut them to the ground, cultivate, fertilize, and water. The foliage that grew back was clean, and the flowers, though late, were as lovely as ever. It did mean, however, that I had to do a lot of emergency moving of plants to camouflage the temporarily empty spaces.

I know the conventional solution given by respected professionals and it must have taken care of the mildew problem for them. All I can say is that for me it hasn't. We are told to keep plants some distance apart for good circulation of air, to thin clumps to two or three shoots per plant, and to spray early in the season with a fungicide. One year, though, I had close-planted masses of phlox, with no mildew, while widely spaced plants in the nursery beds were turned white by it. So now you know exactly what to do, don't you?

Occasionally, after lectures, in frustration at the sameness of questions about phlox, I have suggested Bakalar's three steps for dealing with mildew. 1. Pretend you can't see it (this lasts a day or two); 2. Pretend you like it— "Just look at the woolly white leaves on that phlox, how pretty" (good for another day or two); 3. Cut the whole darn thing down (problem solved: the next growth will be clean).

Presumably, all gardeners want the same thing for their phlox—strong plants, glorious colors, lustrous, healthy leaves and—one more thing—a long period of bloom. Careful deadheading can go a long way toward this.

Deadhead phlox in stages, from light cuttings to complete cutting down. Begin by removing small clusters of flowers as they fade; next, remove the whole panicle, or truss, cutting to the first leaf node below it. Lateral flower buds will appear at the node, and after they fade it is time to cut the stems all the way down to the base of the plant. You may choose to give soluble plant food at this stage, if you wish, but in any case aeration and careful watering will speed up rebloom.

It's just as well to keep phlox deadheaded because they're generous self-seeders, and the volunteers are often that undistinguished, muddy pink that people complain about, muttering darkly about their phlox plants "reverting to magenta." The original plants don't "revert," but the seedlings are highly variable and a good many will be that unpopular color. Phlox bloom at different times, so with a good selection of cultivars there will be some in bloom at all times. The earliest bloomers for me (after 'Miss Lingard') are 'Tenor' (rose red) and 'Starfire' (orange red). Among the latest are 'Eva Cullum' (heavy wine pink) and 'World Peace' (white).

This late-blooming antique phlox, with no name, is often found surviving in old New England gardens. Slim, sharply pointed buds open to small white flowers with a purple eye.

But wait, there is still one more to come. I found a budded phlox in an old garden, early one October. The petals were wrapped spiral fashion, in their buds. There was a glimpse of rich purple. The buds opened to small, pure white flowers with that same purple in the eye. I moved some into my garden. They have incredibly thick, strong stems and bloom so late that I don't deadhead. In some years I have put the rest of the garden to bed in late October and left it for the winter, with that beautiful thing still blooming, still heavily budded. So, if you inherit an old garden, or visit an abandoned one, keep an eye open for one special phlox that may have survived over the years. Take a piece for your garden, by all means, but leave some for others.

$\mathcal{A}$LL THE OTHER STUFF—ANNUALS, BULBS, CORMS, ETC.

Real gardeners don't look at their gardens and say, "There! That's that! Finished!" Or, if they do, they only mean: "For this year."

For one thing, the garden has an organic life of its own and is changing all the time. For another, the gardener is changing too, acquiring more knowledge, gaining more experience, and—a bit more subtle, this—almost imperceptibly changing in his or her own taste. What is satisfying one year isn't the next, but perhaps this is all to the good.

The treasure trove of plants available to gardeners is enormous and increasing year by year. Seduced by pictures and reports of so many lovely things, the gardener steps outside the limits of what is hardy and grows tender plants for summer beauty—anything that will add to the palette. Enough is not enough, apparently. And certainly not to people whose winters are as long as, though they seem longer than, their summers. They add and add to their "perennial" borders, enriching them with tender annuals, with exotic flowers that grow from bulbs and tubers, and with plants whose glory is chiefly in their foliage. Everything is grist to their mill.

Annuals in the Late-summer Garden

The concentration, so far, has been on perennials for late summer color, but few gardeners would deny the contribution annuals have to make to the overall scene. Leaving aside the standard fare in annuals, which is available everywhere in early summer, there are later-blooming annuals that will provide novelty, energy, and glorious color when they come into bloom in August—just in time, I might add, since with even the most devoted attention, an all-perennial planting can look as if it needs a rest at about this time.

Occasionally a visitor will walk around my garden and, pointing, say almost disapprovingly, "Isn't that an annual?" I suppose that's because mine is thought of as a perennial garden. It's true that I grow more perennials than annuals but I find that they complement each other beautifully and I need and grow both. I'm no purist; I embrace everything that can add to the repertoire (exception: I have never embraced a flowering cabbage).

Consider the ways in which annuals can not only come to the gardener's rescue but improve and enliven the garden. Annuals can be seeded around a young, small perennial to cover the space that must be left for its eventual size, or around an established perennial whose disappearance into summer dormancy will leave a large hole. These are two situations that you can expect and plan for. Think of a third, and unexpected, situation: a choice plant, one that you were counting on, dies or otherwise disappears. With annuals growing in reserve for just such an emergency, you could transplant enough to fill the void.

By midsummer, the oriental poppy that was such a glowing feature of the June border is either a sorry mound of yellowed leaves or has disappeared altogether into dormancy, as has an earlier beauty, bleeding heart. Either will have left a sizable hole. Knowing that this would happen, you might have seeded something like annual baby's breath around the poppy, or annual candytuft around the bleeding heart. You didn't? Then you could now go to your rows of annuals growing in reserve and transplant what you need. You didn't seed there, either? In that case, it's off to your local nursery and hope they haven't sold out, and make a note to grow a few reserve annuals next year.

Ideally, there will be space somewhere in the garden to grow these "understudies." I seed them between rows in the vegetable garden. Many annuals will transplant easily, but a few can be tricky. Forget poppies, for instance, and insubstantial plants such as baby's breath and love-in-a-mist, for these are successful only when sown where they are to grow. Choose annuals that can be moved easily without loss. The following "understudy" annuals are among my major standbys; I use them because they tolerate transplanting in midsummer:

- For the back of the border or where height is needed: white sunflower (*Helianthus annuus*) 'Italian White'; cosmos (*Cosmos bipinnatus*) 'Purity' (white), 'Dazzler' (deep red).
- Midborder: heliotrope (*Heliotropium arborescens*) 'Marine'; tobacco flower (*Nicotiana alata*) (white or various colors).
- Front of border: blanketflower (*Gaillardia pulchella*) 'Red Plume' (deep brick red); candytuft (*Iberis amara*) 'White Rocket'; globe candytuft (*Iberis umbellata*) (mixed colors).
- Border's edge: white zinnia (*Zinnia angustifolia*).

Annuals are more than a last resort; they offer an unbelievable variety of flower form and color. In many annuals the overall plant does not have a lot to recommend it. The foliage may be sparse and the form itself lax; the flower is everything. But, remember, there will be plenty of perennials with excellent form sitting about in the border doing nothing, either out of, or not yet in, bloom. What could be better than to use them as partners for colorful annuals?

I have enjoyed seeing painted tongues (*Salpiglossis sinuata*) against a Kansas gayfeather (*Liatris spicata*) that will not bloom again but still holds the dusty spikes of July's flowers; also love-in-a-mist (*Nigella damascena*) in rich bloom against the leggy stems of a white balloon flower (*Platycodon grandiflorum*). On a larger scale, Mexican sunflower (*Tithonia rotundifolia*) looks wonderful next to plume poppy (*Macleaya cordata*).

Other possibilities for good combinations of annuals and perennials might include:

- California poppy (*Eschscholzia californica*) in brightest orange, facing down a sea holly (*Eryngium alpinum*) in metallic blue.
- Spider flower (*Cleome hasslerana*) 'Violet Queen' behind pale mauve *Phlox paniculata* 'Franz Schubert'.
- Pot marigold (*Calendula officinalis*), in lemon or apricot shades, against a blue-violet balloon flower (*Platycodon mariesii*).

But I don't want to spoil your fun by listing any more here—gardeners are entitled to an opportunity to dream and try out their own original combinations.

There is one annual (well, it's grown as an annual in colder parts of the country) that has strong form, handsome foliage, and comes in various rich colors—snapdragon (*Antirrhinum majus*). It can hold its own with any perennial, and I reserve space for it every year. The first blooms on snapdragons are magnificent and, cut back, they will bloom again by late August or September. They do even better in cool weather, responding with thick, strong stems and solid flower spikes, and they can survive frost in October.

The best thing about growing annuals is that every year brings another chance. You can try something new, repeat something successful, or, after a particularly unfortunate summer, decide you never want to see a certain plant in your garden again.

Bulbs, Corms, and Tubers for the Late-summer Garden

Sometimes, when visitors "ooh" and "ah" over bold dahlias, giant summer hyacinths, and fragrant, mysterious acidanthera, I catch myself saying apologetically, "Oh, those—I can't take credit for them. I just plant them and that's what they do." For a long time, I thought it was cheating to grow such easy flowers. It is, after all, simply a matter of planting them in early summer, lifting them in fall, and storing them over the winter. But where is it written that everything has to be difficult?

Growing these extravagant-looking flowers is the closest you'll come to instant gratification in the garden. You can plan ahead and order by mail, or you can go to a garden store as late as May (but try in March or April for a better selection) and buy dahlia tubers, gladiolus corms, and summer hyacinth bulbs. Most are native to the warmer growing areas of the world, and in colder climes must be grown between frost dates. Planted in the garden at the end of May, they'll give you glorious flowers from August until frost. Add to this the fact that they double or triple in quantity each season, and you have a collection of unbeatable plants.

Unkind things have been said about dahlias, most often about the enormous show blooms the size of dinner plates, so heavy and tall that they have to be rigidly tied to strong stakes. Even so, lashed to the mast, as it were, the huge heads still hang downward and after rain they're a depressing sight. But dahlias come in a wonderful range of size, shape, and color, and there's something for everybody.

I like my dahlias in modest sizes. A favorite for many years has been the cactus-flowered 'Park Princess', with rolled petals like quills, in rich pink. Another, more

The cactus-flowered dahlia, 'Park Princess', glows in the September border, with more than enough blooms for cutting.

dramatic, dahlia is 'Arabian Nights'. This is a taller plant whose three-inch flowers are in a smoky red so dark as to look black against the sky. I've enjoyed this in one part of the garden behind a second bloom of blue scabiosa and, in a shadier spot, with the pristine white Japanese anemone 'Honorine Jobert'.

I don't find storing the tubers too tiresome, and the rate at which they multiply gives me plenty to spread around and "pass along."

Gladiolus, it seems, is one man's meat and another man's poison. The tall ones are hard to use gracefully, and are better grown in the cutting garden. But there are miniatures that will provide small pools of color in the late border, and the narrow, upright foliage is itself an attractive feature. My favorite in this family, though not a true gladiolus, is the so-called Abyssinian gladiolus (*Acidanthera*). The long-throated white flowers are blotched with chocolate-brown. It has a delicious fragrance and smells every bit as exotic as it looks.

Even more exotic, though without the fragrance, is the tiger or Mexican shell flower (*Tigridia*). Its vivid, spotted petals in yellow, red, and orange shades are of such brilliance that I would have expected the hummingbirds to be all over it. But they pass it by. North of Zone 6, the corms of all three of these late beauties must be dug and stored.

A more modest flower, though not in size, is the giant summer hyacinth (*Galtonia candicans*). Above the low, strappy foliage, flowers are held on strong stems, two to three feet tall, that hold up well on their own. The pendulous white bells are arranged in a spike. Although every reference mentions galtonia's fragrance—and certainly the common name leads one to expect it—it has so far eluded me. Galtonia bulbs multiply generously and, like the corms and tubers, store easily over the winter.

I was surprised one July day, visiting a famous garden in England, to see a number of empty spaces in a border. With heavy support stakes already driven in, and labels bearing the names of dahlias and other glamour plants (a sort of "Coming Attractions in the Garden") I wondered whether breathless anticipation of the glories yet to come was supposed to compensate for those ugly holes. In my case it didn't, but how delicious to be able to criticize a great and famous garden instead of being eaten up with envy of it!

I recommend discretion in the use of these bold plants; just because they're available doesn't mean that you have to use all of them or endure empty spaces to save room for their later appearance. A few will light up the border; too many make a riot. It's far better, in my opinion (and I acknowledge that there's a lot of that here), to have much of the border moving naturally and gently from summer into fall.

I have a picture in my mind of my favorite part of a late October border, where some of the loveliest passages are provided not by flowers at all but by form and foliage. Peonies continue to offer good form, their leaves coloring to a rich autumnal red. A five-foot candelabrum of yellow mullein (*Verbascum bombyciferum*) leans into an oak-leafed hydrangea. Hosta leaves, nearly translucent, pale to a ghostly parchment color. The narrow gray-green leaves of a small blue willow hold cobwebs and in the cobwebs, raindrops.

Day by day, there is change. Some leaves deepen in color, some fade; others relinquish their hold and, falling, make a pool of amber on the ground. A few plants remain at attention: a tall leafless coneflower holds one brown cone atop a stem dry and strong as a bamboo stake, while nearby, *Sedum* 'Autumn Joy' stands ready to catch the first snows on its copper flower heads, and the garden moves inevitably on its way toward winter.

CHAPTER 11

. . . .

JOYS AND CHORES

*I*f this chapter had been headed "Summer Garden Maintenance," you would have known immediately what it contained. You might also have decided it was all about deadheading or—worse—weeding, and you didn't care to read any further. "Maintenance" sounds so deadening, so unlike what I do to keep a garden looking beautiful all summer, that I'm reserving the word for lawn mowers and washing machines. Hence "Joys and Chores."

Joyless labor on monotonous tasks has nothing to do with what goes on in my garden. Mind you, this doesn't mean there aren't times when I want to throw in the trowel and storm into the house looking for sympathy. Nobody in her right mind enjoys a sudden cloud of June blackflies when she's halfway through seeding a row, or a violent windstorm just as a showpiece delphinium is almost but not quite tied up, or unexpected sleet out of nowhere (in October, for heaven's sake!) in the middle of seed gathering. These are life's awful moments in the garden, and although I mean it when I say I enjoy doing all the things involved in gardening, there are a few I enjoy less than others.

So what is involved in keeping a flower garden going through the summer? The first thing that comes to many minds is weeding, but let's keep a sense of proportion here. Ask a few people who obviously don't like gardening what their objections to it are. I'm willing to bet that they'll begin with a diatribe against weeding. Another thing I'll bet on is that as hapless children those people were sent out to weed carrots—endless rows of tiny feathery carrots—and they didn't even *like* carrots.

To get back to the tasks necessary to keep a flower garden going through summer, they are: cutting back and deadheading; edging; moving plants; staking;

watching for insects and disease; watering and feeding; weeding. Since all these tasks are common to gardens everywhere, I'll describe each one before going on to tell you how I tackle them in my own garden.

We'll assume that much of the flower garden is in place and in order, and that this program of summer upkeep begins around the first week in June. (Spring garden work before that date is described in *Your Garden in Spring,* page 50.)

CUTTING BACK

Some plants grow so tall and lanky that they look out of proportion in the border. The remedy is cutting back. Early in summer, when they are about two feet tall, shear back by about one third their length the shoots of asters such as 'Harrington's Pink' and heleniums like 'Butterpat'. It results in a bushier-shaped plant, and prevents their shooting up to a leggy six or seven feet, with all their flowers held at one level, practically out of sight. Make the cuts lowest on the outside stems and gradually higher as you get to the center. This results in a rounded shape. The technique is most effective on multistemmed plants like asters, heleniums, and the boltonia 'Snowbank'.

Just remember, you will be cutting off potential flowering shoots, so do it early enough in the season for the plant to set more flower buds and bloom before frost date. I've used the *Aster* 'Harrington's Pink' as a guinea pig in my summer workshops. Some were cut back once, carefully, at the right time; others, less carefully, and several times, by different students. As a result, these aster plants began to bloom at several different times, and at several different heights. The unlucky one in the front that had received the most frequent attention from the most students didn't bloom at all.

DEADHEADING

Deadheading is removing flower heads as they fade. There are two reasons for doing this. One is principally cosmetic, to improve the appearance of the plant, most often a perennial; the other, much more important, reason is to prevent the plant from setting seed. It is particularly important to deadhead annuals if you want them to keep on blooming (and why else would you be growing them?).

A true annual goes through its complete life cycle in one year. It comes into life from seed, blooms, sets seed, and dies. Once an annual has set seed it loses interest in the whole business of making flowers; its mission accomplished, it quits.

Watch what you're doing when you deadhead; a "helper" of mine, deadheading a big patch of petunias, pulled off all the flower petals very neatly, leaving the seeds forming at the base of the receptacle.

In addition to removing individual spent flowers, it's a good idea to cut back whole stems and sprays, to encourage fresh, bushy growth lower down on the plant. I do this with pansies, petunias, heliotrope, and any other annuals that get leggy.

EDGING

If you do this job right when you first lay out the flower bed or border, it won't be difficult to keep up. When a border is edged with paving stone or brick, the plants in front can be allowed to flop over onto it. In fact, lavender, catnip, and other herbs of that shape look their best this way, and soften what might otherwise be a hard edge. But flower beds are more often bordered by grass walks.

Mounding the soil slightly improves drainage. The slight trench exposes the cut turf edge and inhibits its creeping growth into flower beds.

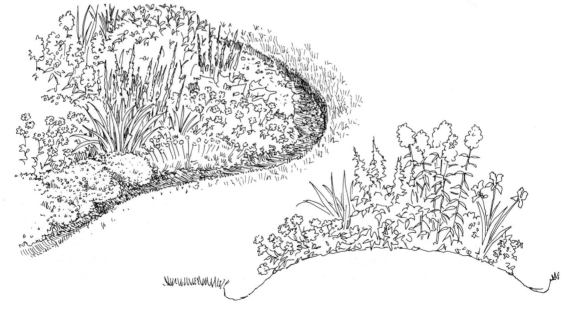

The grass, the clover, and every other weed in that turf, all head for the good stuff—the enriched soil of your flower bed, and a long battle threatens. Before I got serious about edging, I discovered that in one season I could lose from six to nine inches of flower border to encroaching grass.

You can buy edging by the yard: from the cheapest, which is shiny, ugly metal, to the most expensive, a heavy-duty, dark plastic with a rolled-top edge. A determined teenager with a heavy machine can mow either of them to pieces, however, so I don't use either.

When you first construct your flower bed, cut down deeply along or around the edges with a spade (a *spade*, not a shovel) or, if you want to be fancy, a steel edger. Either will do a good job. Mound up the soil slightly onto the bed, leaving a small trench to expose the cut edge of the turf and inhibit its creeping growth. Don't overdo this. An unnaturally wide band of bare earth will make it look like a municipal war memorial.

I don't believe in having a neat, regimented garden, but we do have quite a few visitors, and I've discovered something interesting. The flower beds can be groomed to within an inch of their lives, the edges left somewhat woolly and wavy, and visitors aren't particularly laudatory in their remarks about the garden. But really crisp edging around a not-so-tidy flower bed seems always to evoke extravagantly favorable comment. So, whatever it is about edges, and if you care about appearances, you know what to do the day before: get out there and edge. My garden helpers and I joke about this, but we do it.

*M*OVING AND REMOVING

The basic procedure of moving plants from one place to another is described in How I Plant (see *Moving Plants Around,* page 96). What I hope to do here is to charge you up to fly in the face of much conventional wisdom about moving plants. After all, aren't we told to move late-blooming plants in spring and early-blooming plants in fall? Here I am about to urge you to indulge yourself by moving any plant whenever you see clearly a place where it would look better. And this puts plant-moving right in there with summer jobs, even if it isn't strictly upkeep.

To my mind, this is one of the very best parts of flower gardening—all joy, no chore. Imagine you are walking around your garden and you notice that one of a handsome group of phloxes, in full bloom, has grown too big and is not the color you expected. In fact, you don't like it there at all, but it would be perfect in another group that needs that color to give it life. Divide it and move it!

Out in the garden just before dusk, you notice the luminous blues in the lovely Siberian iris 'Sea Shadows'. Snapping off a flower stalk you take it and, for the sheer pleasure it gives you, you rest it on a mound of lady's mantle. Voilà—a perfect combination in both color and form. Move the iris!

A daylily you thought would be just right in front of yellow meadow rue has grown a lot; suddenly, it looks too dense, too substantial, and out of scale. The space it leaves may do more for that part of the garden than the daylily itself ever did. Move it!

It's not spring, it's not fall, it's early July. You're supposed to "make a note to move it in fall." But when fall comes, there's everything to do; it runs a close second to spring for work. Besides, are you sure you'll be able to find that reminder, written so confidently in July, and will it seem as important then as it does today? Move it now!

As gardeners we have to spend a lot of time waiting, containing ourselves with patience, while some fussy treasure makes up its mind whether to grow, bloom, or die. I think we're entitled to some instant gratification. If it must be truly instant, go ahead but if you can wait one day, here's what you do to guarantee the safety of the moving operation:

In the evening, thoroughly water the plant you're going to move. I believe this is the most important step. It needs overnight to soak in, so that next day the soil will hold together in a solid mass. Prepare a hole for its new home, not forgetting to put compost in the bottom, and water that too. Next morning, effect the move. Dig all around the plant, lifting it in a good chunk of soil, and carry it carefully to the prepared hole. Set it in at the same level it was before. Fill in any spaces with good soil. Firm and water in thoroughly, but gently, adding soluble fertilizer. Shade from sun and wind for a day or two.

*S*UPPORTING THE WEAK

Visitors often ask why my plants are standing up and theirs are flopping or prostrate. They sound quite cross, and I don't blame them. I sometimes wonder if decency doesn't require me to knock a few down before they arrive.

First of all, I tell them, do what you can to reduce the need for support. Good planting in good soil is important. Compost or other nutrients below the plant encourage roots to go deeper for moisture, giving the plant a firm grip on the soil. Beyond this:

- Try not to put tall, top-heavy plants in a windy location (impossible in my hillside garden, where wind is a constant).
- Surround the "wobblers" with lower, stronger plants that will hold them up. This is aesthetically pleasing as well as practical.
- Don't try to grow plants that need full sun in a shady spot.
- Cut tall perennials back early in the season, so that they won't carry all their flowers in a top-heavy mass.

All this will help but you'll still be left with some that need a firmer hand (or shoulder). I'll leave stakes and staking to last, because I regard it as a last resort. Also, there's something about the very word stake that reminds me of the gorier parts of long-ago history lessons.

One easy support system that I use strikes many garden students as novel, which surprises me. When I was growing up "pea brush" was the foundation of

A pile of pea brush, cut and ready for spring. Pushed in among newly planted annuals, it provides support but is soon hidden by the growing plants.

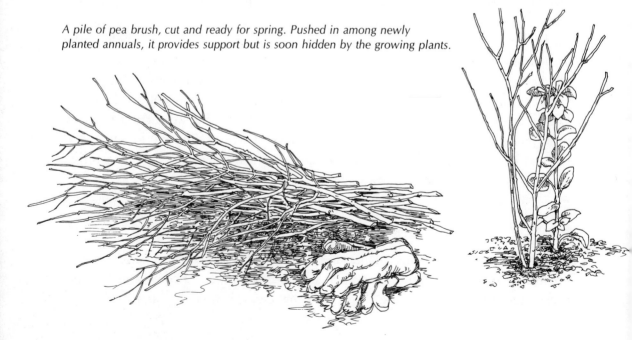

every weak plant or clump of plants. It was dry branches and twigs, often hedge clippings, pushed in as the plants emerged or the seedlings were transplanted in spring. I haven't heard it called pea brush here, so I just say brush, or hedge brush. The name comes from its common use in England as support for green peas. I tried it early in my vegetable gardening days—sowed two rows of peas, cut twigs from hedges, and pushed them in between the rows. All the peas rotted that cold, wet spring. Every piece of brush rooted. Try to cut your brush the year before, but in any case be sure you're using old twigs.

There's a great deal of hardhack and weedy shrub material along the edges of the pasture below my garden. I try to go on a cutting expedition in the fall, piling the clippings in some out-of-the-way place over winter. At the same time I look for tall, thin, straight branches, and a few forked ones. I use brush for many annuals, including love-in-a-mist, tobacco flowers, nicotiana, and snapdragons, and for a few perennials, notably the summer aster (*Aster × frikartii*), the floppy veronica, 'Crater Lake', and the leggy scabiosa.

Hedge and shrub clippings ("pea brush") will provide strong but inconspicuous support for annuals and small perennials.

I think persuasion is better than force with plants. When a high wind makes a bushy plant flop over to one side, I gather it up and push in a strong stake behind it to hold it upright. I don't tie it. Many times this does the trick and I'm able to remove the stake in a day or two. I won't dwell on the occasions when the wind has changed on me and blown plant, stakes, and all in the opposite direction. When that happens, the next step is either cut the plant down (bad temper!), or enclose it in a stockade of low stakes held together with twine (better idea!).

I find the stockade technique the most practical for peonies. Foliage on

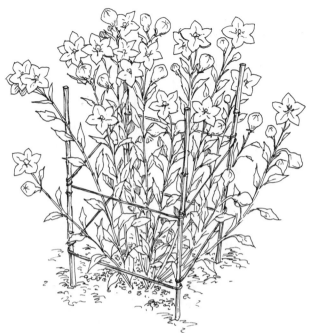

A border clematis that grows to a 4' × 4' bush every summer needs a strong stockade of stakes and twine.

A mature platycodon will often splay outward unless supported. Bamboo stakes and inconspicuous twine make this stockade.

these wonderful plants is strong throughout the whole season; it's the heavy-headed flowers that fall. I've heard people say that they like peonies but won't grow them because it's impossible to keep the flowers off the ground. Oh, come on (or pull yourself together, as my famous aunt would say), you can find a way. I myself don't like to see the gorgeous double heads of the peony 'Festiva Maxima' hanging over the top of a stockade, so in addition I often prop individual flowers up on a forked branch. The minute the flowers are past, I take down all supports and there's the peony again, its own beautiful, strong, shrublike self.

There's another plant, the pink balloon flower, the one that grows taller than the blues or whites, that does better supported by a stockade. Put in early enough, and with a few stems left outside for a more natural effect, the stockade is not visible.

There's nothing for it, I see I have arrived at staking. I grow the tall *Delphinium elatum* from seed, trying different colors each year. Most of them bloom in a production garden in their first year, and there they can be staked for safety, and never mind esthetics.

Once I put them in the border, however, they are a significant element in its design, and their role requires them to stand tall and look queenly, which is difficult when tied by the neck to a thick bamboo of the wrong color.

Delphinium will need your time and patience if they are to fulfill this role. A broken spire is a sad sight. You can be sure that wherever the stake ends, that's where the stem will snap. Now is the time for the tallest stakes you can buy. Bamboos and green plastic stakes come in six- and seven-foot lengths, but the thickness increases in proportion to the length. Try for the longest and thinnest.

Better even than any of these, find a few pliable, wandlike branches for a more natural effect. I cut long shoots from osier dogwood. (But be careful— it roots before your very eyes.) The advantage is that as a support it gives a little with the wind. A six-foot delphinium is one foot foliage and five feet flowering stem. I make the first tie just above the basal foliage. From there up to the very top, it needs three ties, maybe even four.

Normally more level-headed, I have gone all out on a few critical occasions, making figure-eight ties around the delicate stems, with French tapestry wool in matching green. This is supposed to be a book of helpful, practical suggestions and I can't honestly justify the tapestry wool bit. But since confession is so good for the soul, I will admit to one more thing. When, despite all the staking and tying, a prize delphinium (to be the star of that day's Significant Occasion) snapped near the base, I stuffed wet tissues in the hollow stem and taped the two ends together. It held up for the rest of the day. If all this sounds like too much, forget the tall delphiniums and grow the shorter 'Blue Fountain' series, which are only about three feet tall.

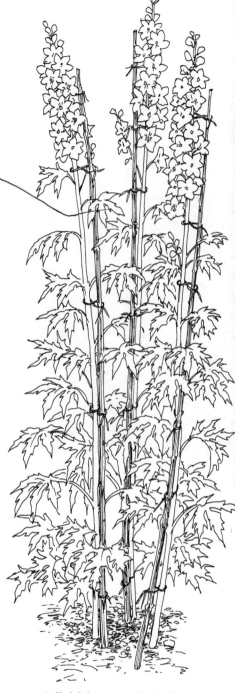

Tall delphinium calls for the longest, thinnest stakes you can find. Figure-eight ties are kindest to the stems.

*Tall hybrid delphinium need tall
thin stakes, and tying is fussy work.*

For the front of the border, try the dwarf *Delphinium grandiflorum* 'Blue Butterflies'. It's not dependably perennial, but it will bloom in its first year from seed. Plant in groups of six or more, and enjoy the richly blue flowers on one-and-a-half-foot stems. Short hedge brush is all these plants need for support.

If you don't get around in time to putting supports in place and later find plants lying on the ground, don't be too eager to pull them upright. For one thing, they're likely to snap; for another, any flower buds that have set in the leaf axils along the fallen stems will forever arise at an odd angle when the plant is pulled upright. Snapdragons sometimes get away from me in this way. I find it best to draw the long fallen stems forward between other plants and enjoy the bonus of unexpected sprigs of color along the ground.

A WATCHFUL EYE

Fascinating as some insects are, I don't suggest great hunting expeditions for the relatively few troublemakers. All that's needed is a watchful eye as you go on your usual garden rounds. I have a fairly watchful eye, but I know when to turn a blind eye, too. I've described elsewhere my somewhat laissez faire attitude to mildew, and I suppose this goes to some extent for many of the insects that seem to get other gardeners excited.

I can't see running around the garden spraying poison on everything. I am lazy about spraying in general, so my decision is part principle, part sloth. No awful damage is done; many insect invasions and fungus and disease outbreaks are brief and occur at only one stage in the summer, not to be repeated on later growth.

Spittle bugs—their white froth is called "cuckoo spittle" in England—have never seemed to harm the plants they hide in. Japanese beetles are not sufficiently numerous to justify or excuse hanging those awful traps around the garden. Those traps have to be emptied, too, and I'd rather take the beetles off by hand.

Each year, legions of aphids descend on the lupins, fortunately not until the flowers have faded, so at that point I cut the plants down, putting the foliage in a bag for later disposal at the dump. I have no idea where the aphids go; surely some escape, but I've never seen them on other plants, and the new foliage on the lupins is always clean.

I must admit, there is one insect pest that gets me excited enough to make up for all the others that don't. Day after day, I used to find columbine plants with fewer leaves, but no sign of an enemy. In another day or so, the plants would be totally defoliated and shortly thereafter totally dead. It's

Baby's breath grows in a large, billowing cloud that will soon hide the tomato cage used here for support. Leaving a few stems outside each ring gives a more natural effect.

not so bad now I know what it is and how to deal with it, thanks to a knowledgeable nurseryman who told me it was the larva of a small moth called a columbine skipper. It's a quarter-inch long, light green caterpillar, almost invisible as it wraps itself around the edge of the leaf it so exactly matches. No more laissez faire, no more nice guy. Fortunately, there is an organic solution. I spray the foliage every two weeks with *B.t.* (*Bacillus thuringiensis*).

A few things still puzzle me: Why couldn't I see it until it was described to me? Why hadn't I read a word about this problem? All the literature describes columbine as being susceptible to leaf miner, a problem I don't have; and last, why doesn't the label on *B.t.* include this columbine pest among the many caterpillars it is effective against? If you love columbines as much as I do, I hope you know this already, or will now be prepared to deal with it.

WATERING

General anxiety about the decrease in annual rainfall over much of the country is already having one good result—a more thoughtful approach to the use of water. All too often, watering the garden is something people do because water is available.

Obviously, plants need water, but do they need as much as they are given? I water any plant copiously when I first plant it and at any time I move it. For the rest, I keep an eye on the garden and water only those plants that appear in need.

Without sufficient humus, soil dries out quickly after rain or watering. But if you've prepared your soil carefully, added a lot of humus, and set your plants on a good footing of compost, moisture will be held there, within reach of the roots.

That takes care of the situation underground. What about the surface, and water loss through evaporation? Well, mulching gets almost as much attention today as composting, but before going any further, I'd better tell you that I don't mulch my flower beds. I mulch shrub plantings and young trees, and I mulch raspberry and blueberry plantings, but flower beds, never. For one thing, I don't like the look of flowers against mulch, and for another, my "stuff-and-cram" borders don't leave room for much bare earth. When they did, in the first year, I knew it wasn't forever and I chose to weed instead of mulching. As the perennials grew in size, any bare earth disappeared. The leaf canopy served two purposes, shading the ground and keeping it moist, and inhibiting the growth of weeds. I do sometimes mulch a few plants for winter protection, but I use what's free— and around here that's pine needles. It makes sense to use what is locally available since transportation adds so much to the cost.

We have gone from the watering can to the watering system, and a highly sophisticated system it is. Any good garden supply catalog now includes a veritable arsenal of such equipment. Much of it has been designed to encourage gardeners to get water to the roots of plants, where it is most effectively used, without sending it wildly over the garden, some of it to evaporate en route and some to leave wet foliage prone to the spread of disease.

Even without the high-tech stuff, you can apply the principles to your own garden. From experience, I know it is true that if you're the one who has to lug buckets of water to the garden, you make sure that it goes only to plants that need it, and you apply it to their roots. A hose is very handy for moving water to the place where it's needed but it can tempt the gardener and, particularly, the nongardener into standing there for hours waving it about in great airy sweeps over the garden. Give such a friend a soaker hose to keep him or her out of trouble.

SHOPPING FOR MULCH

Go to any sizable garden center and you're likely to find labeled bins of mulches from which you can make your choice. Your purse may steer you away from buckwheat hulls, the aristocrat of mulches, and your nose, probably, from cocoa-bean hulls. (I hope you won't linger over the bins of glistening white or—even worse—multicolored stone chips.)

Then there are the free or low-cost mulches. In many rural areas, hay and straw will be available, but watch out for all the grass and weed seeds, especially in fresh hay. There is the same problem with compost as mulch if the temperature in the pile has not been high enough to kill the seeds (see *Using Compost,* page 45).

Shredded paper is sometimes used as a mulch by home gardeners, but you may not like the look of it and it has a tendency to blow about the garden.

Given the quantity of leaves falling on many yards in autumn, a leaf mulch is an obvious choice. Composted or not, shredded leaves look attractive, break down quickly, and, in addition, provide nutrients to the soil as they do so.

Do not use peat moss as a mulch. I mention it here only because there's some confusion about its function. It's a good soil additive but hopeless, and possibly dangerous as a mulch. When dry it either blows away or compacts to a water-repelling mass, like a mat of coconut fiber; it can even catch fire.

*F*EEDING

Assuming that there is compost under most plants and that spring transplants received soluble plant food when they were watered in, there will be little need for much feeding during the summer. In general, perennials will not need feeding now, although some, like delphinium, that make a second flush of foliage and flowers, should get a boost of something after the first cutting down (see *The Garden in Late Summer,* page 138).

Annuals are another matter. Their life will be spent by the end of the season, so you can push them to maximum bloom by giving them a fertilizer high in phosphates. A commercial fertilizer with the formula 5-10-5 or 10-20-10, for instance, would give you nitrogen, phosphate, and potassium, in a 1-2-1 ratio.

What you give them, organic or inorganic, is up to you, but you should know that organic fertilizers such as fish emulsion, seaweed extract, and manure tea—all excellent over time—are slow-acting. This is the time for the quick boost that a chemical fertilizer can give.

*W*EEDING

Don't get caught up in all the horror talk about weeding. It's not bad at all. I enjoy it (me—with my childhood garden experience!); it may even be habit-forming, in which case there's a danger you'll have the urge to weed and there'll be no weeds left. Imagine that predicament!

There are one or two things about weeds that it pays to remember. The bad news is that, unchecked, they increase year by year—annual weeds by seed, perennial weeds by seed plus many vegetative means. Weeds may be Nature's mulch, as a determined nonweeder once put it, but they're greedy mulches, with roots that will get more than a fair share of the moisture and nutrients your chosen plants need.

The good news is that as you garden—sensibly—there will be fewer and fewer weeds each year. Any gardener who has worked on a piece of ground for a number of years will confirm that.

New gardeners often get a flourishing crop of weeds in their flower beds because they can't distinguish between germinating weeds and flower plants. You'll learn a lot from observation and experience, but it's a good idea to find a book and get familiar with a few of the villainous weeds in your area. If your neighbors are experienced gardeners, they will be glad to identify some of them for you.

The trick with annual weeds is to catch them before they set seed: "One year's seeding, seven years weeding," as the old adage has it. Hoe or "scuffle" them up while they're young and small, and they'll wither and die on the soil's surface. Don't do this in rain because anything left lying on the surface will reroot.

Among perennial weeds, dandelion and dock are probably on every gardener's Most Wanted list. Both have strong, deep taproots, and you must dig deeply enough to get the whole thing or your efforts will be wasted. In tight corners and among stones, the deep weeder hand tool is effective on these and other taprooted weeds. Remember that any weed, annual or perennial, is easily destroyed when it is young. So when you spot one, no matter how small, don't delay.

A friend of mine who had a full-time job, as well as what should have been a full-time garden, told me she began by making herself pull six weeds as she left the house each morning. In a few days' time she was pulling twenty or thirty, and found it so compelling that she could hardly stop. She swears she enjoyed it.

I don't like to use weed killers, although I understand, of course, that there are situations that may warrant their use. Poison ivy in a garden or play area would justify it, I imagine. At all costs, avoid indiscriminate spraying with all-purpose, kill-everything chemicals. Be selective. Be conservative. And be careful.

$\mathcal{E}$*NJOYING*

The tasks above constitute quite a list, but I don't mean to suggest that that's all there is to gardening in the summer—just another list of jobs to be taped to the refrigerator door, a daily reminder of things to do.

You're going to be in your garden every day in summer. Even if you go off to a daily job, I'm sure you'll be out there first thing in the morning, in the afternoon or early evening when you come home, and, I hope, at dusk, the most magical time in a garden. And you will be doing what is one of the most important things a gardener does. You will be *looking*. The rewards are immeasurable.

Give up any thought of grinding your way around the whole garden working on one single task. It's tedious in the extreme and with such a narrow focus you'll miss all kinds of interesting things going on around you. Just think—by the time you've got the whole way around on the first task, it's time to start at the beginning again. What an awful thought. Instead, I'm suggesting that you give yourself up to the enjoyment of one small area in your garden and do whatever you see needs to be done there.

*A*N HOUR IN THE GARDEN

Let me show you what I mean by describing what I see and what I do for an hour in the border on a day in July. I take a small cart or a carryall of some kind with the tools and supplies that I think I'll need. I find a way into the border—it might be at either end or it might be smack in the middle—but it will be a section I find myself drawn to. Right in front of me, in the part I have chosen, is a mound of cottage pinks. The flowers are dry and brown. I clip off a good bit of foliage as well as the dead flower heads; the new growth will be a fresh blue-green.

I deadhead some beautiful columbines next to it—I want to keep them blooming as long as possible. All clippings and weeds go into a bucket or a basket for pickup later and carting to the compost pile.

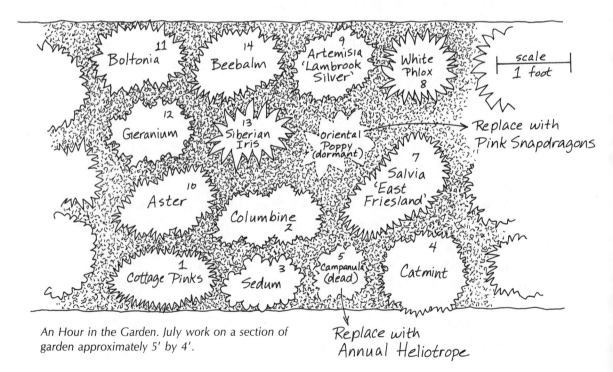

An Hour in the Garden. July work on a section of garden approximately 5' by 4'.

I notice a crop of weeds, tiny but promising, under the leaves of the sedums, and fork over the soil to get rid of them—no problem at this stage.

Further along the front edge, a catnip is in full blush. That's fortunate because alongside it is a campanula, planted too late last fall, that's now definitely dead. I dig it out, work up the soil a bit, and make a note to use that space for annual heliotrope. How am I going to remember that? I take a red-tipped plant label out of my pocket and stick it in there as a place holder and highly visible reminder.

Meanwhile, I draw some sprays of the full catnip plant over the empty space.

Behind these plants is a miserable-looking sight (three weeks ago, it was glorious)—an oriental poppy getting ready to pack it in for the summer. I decide to leave a few big seed heads for effect. The yellowing leaves come away from the crown at a touch, their job finished, and I put them in the compost collection. Between the poppy and the big catmint, a group of young plants of Salvia 'East Friesland' are just opening their purple spikes. They will continue to give color for at least another month.

This is my big chance to remove a deep-rooted dock that's growing right up through the poppy, and I do this with my handy deep weeder. This particular weed can legitimately be called evil; even now I may not have got it all.

What about the big empty space the poppy has left? Snapdragons to the rescue—tall pink ones, in the 'Rocket' series. I put in a dozen or two and give them a boost with soluble fertilizer when I water them. Some small brush (hedge clippings) pushed in among them now will support them as they grow and will soon be quite hidden.

Behind the poppy space an early phlox, 'Miss Lingard', is just beginning to fade. I clip off the top, leaving buds in leaf axils further down the stem, to provide flowers for several more weeks.

There's an aster here, 'Alma Potschke', that I know from experience will be too tall by the time it blooms. I cut back the stems by about one third, keeping the plant to a dome shape. It will bloom in late August.

Behind the aster is a vertical plant with narrow, gray-green leaves, fast getting up to its five-foot height. It's *Boltonia asteroides* 'Snowbank', strong enough to stand on its own and even support other flowers. Good place to transplant a few willowy cosmos plants; 'Radiance', in a deep rose color, will be lovely with boltonia's white asterlike flowers.

Geranium magnificum bore reddish-purple flowers until two weeks ago but

"I've had an hour of enjoyable work. . . ."

will not rebloom. I remove the dead flower stalks and any browned leaves; the remaining attractive rosette of leaves will be handsome well into the fall.

Next to the geranium and in front of a bee balm, the Siberian iris 'White Swirl' was in glistening contrast to both. It, too, will not bloom again, but the leaves will hold up through the summer.

The bee balm, close by, has sent out strong runners like the spokes of a wheel, dense with thick, minty leaves. Already, it's taking too much space, but it's a toughie, so I can take the spade and slice off a clump; I know a place where I can use it. This bee balm makes a big, heavy plant so I cross two green bamboo stakes behind it for support.

A last look around while I'm deep in the border to see if I've missed anything. I work my way out backward, using the small scuffle hoe to cover my footprints. I tidy some grass that has begun to grow in from the edge of the border, and I leave.

I've had an hour of enjoyable work—enjoyable because I've had an opportunity to *look* closely at everything. I feel I know what is going on in that part of the garden; I've attended to its needs and ensured its future beauty. I'm not tired, and I'm eager to move on along the border.

CHAPTER 12

. . . .

FLOWERS FOR CUTTING

*T*o many of us, one of the joys of a garden is having flowers we can cut and bring into the house. There are times, however, when this sets up a conflict. On the day that the balance of color in the border is just about perfect you want some of those same lovely flowers for the house; what are you going to do?

In the best of all possible worlds, there would be that great luxury—a cutting garden full of all the best kinds of flowers for using in the house. Because it would be away from the main garden (and certainly out of sight of the house), there would be no need to keep up appearances. You wouldn't have to bother about the time of bloom, the color harmony (or discord), or the relative height of the plants. The bed could be planted in rows, intensively, leaving only enough space to run a tiller and to get in to cut the flowers. The whole area could be turned under, tilled, fertilized, and rearranged annually. Dreams! Dreams! Cutting gardens like these had their heyday in the Victorian era, when neither space nor labor was a problem.

Back in the real world we are more likely to have to grow our cutting plants in a border that's all too visible, and so must look its best throughout the summer. That offers a challenge, but perhaps it can be done.

To begin with, a cutting garden needs sunshine for the ample production of flowers. This is important in northern gardens, where summer temperatures are moderate; farther south, where they can be very hot, a little less sunshine—even light shade from trees—will do. (Not all the flowers you want for cutting have to be grown in sun. For attractive flowers in a shady spot see *A Garden in the Shade,* page 35.) Soil should be fertile and easily workable, loose in texture and well-drained, yet not so sandy and fast-draining that you are obliged to water constantly to keep the flowers coming.

As for what to grow, this will be the place for a rich palette of annuals with some perennials (fewer in number), to give the bed stability. All should be generous producers of flowers and some should offer interesting seed heads. They should bloom over a long period and hold up well in water when cut. Foliage will be important to hold the bed together since you will be cutting so many of the flowers, and a few deciduous shrubs will serve to give form to the bed and provide branches for cutting.

The shape will depend on the space available, and on the layout of existing beds and borders. If this is to be the only flower bed in a lawn area, you have the widest possible choice. A minimum width of five or six feet will make it easier to keep the bed looking full in spite of the regular removal of flowers. Since you don't have the luxury of that discreetly concealed cutting garden, the arrangement of color has to be carefully considered.

Here are my suggestions for four different-shaped beds. Each can provide flowers for cutting and, at the same time, remain an attractive part of the garden. The following pages may help you make your choice of plants and colors.

Plan A, facing south and toward the house, offers you the opportunity to do a fairly classic border, either in pastel colors or in the brighter, hotter yellows, reds, and bronze colors (see *Flowers for Cutting,* page 188). Your choice will depend on the background and general garden setting.

Since this cutting garden will be seen head-on, as it were, from the house, you might think of unifying a path leading to it and the crescent enclosed by the bed. For once, this might be the right place for a birdbath or sundial. Best of all, however, think how right it would be for a small piece of sculpture. Will you set this on lawn grass, fieldstone, pavers, brick? Your choice.

Plan B is a shade more ambitious (rest assured that once planted it doesn't look so much like a dog's bone or a footprint as it does on the plan). This one will take a lot of plants, but it offers an interesting opportunity to have two "plant climaxes," one in each of the fatter ends of the bed. Although they will need to be large and bold plants, or even colorful shrubs, I suggest restraint and some repetition, to unify this free-form bed.

Plans C and D are wholly utilitarian, being small enough and of a shape to fit into any odd space available (always remembering the need for sunshine). Color in Plan C may be a challenge because of its division into four distinct parts. If you're bold enough, plant the quadrants in four different color schemes. You'll have to decide which color you would like to have facing the house before you begin to plant.

Plan D looks as if it's in a corner, but it's important that the two straight edges should be away from walls or hedges, so as not to impede the sunlight and to provide easy access to the plants.

Because this is not only a cutting garden but also a permanent flower bed, and part of the whole garden, there should be at least a few "important" plants to give it form. If the bed is small, you might rely on big, solid perennials to do this, but remember that in winter there will be nothing left visible. For a larger bed, I suggest one or two shrubs to the rear to provide form that will stand through the winter. Before deciding on an evergreen shrub, think how isolated it might look in winter and, if it is broad-leaved, how much shade it might cast in summer, when the flowers need sunlight. Deciduous shrubs would be better because, even when leafless, they lend some shape to the bed. What's more, some of them might provide a flowering stem, a branch of autumn leaves and, from late fall into winter, a bare twig of interesting shape.

The shape of a bed for growing flowers for cutting depends on the available space and on what is already in the garden. Here are some possibilities.

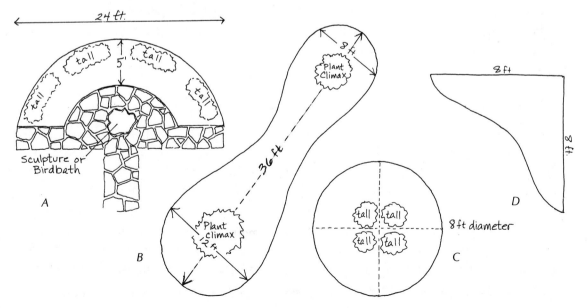

DECIDUOUS SHRUBS

Whatever shrub you choose should have medium or small-sized leaves that will not throw too much shade over the bed or appear too heavy in flower arrangements. For a bed in pastel colors, two of the possibilities are *Spiraea* × *bumalda* 'Anthony Waterer', which blooms June to July at two to three feet, with rose pink flowers; and *Caryopteris clandonensis* 'Blue Mist' (or 'Dark Knight'), which bears fluffy blue flowers in August on a two- to three-foot shrub with small gray-green leaves.

For the center of a bed in hot colors (golden yellow, red, bronze), there is a flowering quince, *Chaenomeles speciosa*, about four feet in height, that blooms March to April, with cultivars in salmon and red. Another, a great favorite of mine, is *Enkianthus campanulatus*, which not only has clusters of red-veined yellow bells on bare stems in April to May, but dazzling orange red foliage in fall. This shrub can grow to twenty feet, but it has been slow-growing in my garden and can, in any case, be kept much lower than that.

PERENNIALS

Although there will usually be fewer perennials than annuals in a cutting garden, they will be significant for the solidity they lend to the bed. In general, the form of the plant will be denser than that of annuals, and the foliage is likely to be an attractive addition. When making your choices, keep in mind that these perennials should have:

- Heavy flower production over a long period;
- Flowers that don't wilt when cut and last long in water;
- Pleasant fragrance (or none);
- Good-looking foliage on strong overall plant form;
- Interesting seed heads (a desirable bonus).

A few big perennials to the rear (or to the center, if it's a circular bed) will go a long way toward anchoring the bed, and will make a substantial background for the changing array of annuals. They will have made good leaf growth while many of the annuals are still at the seedling stage.

Sneezewort (*Helenium autumnale*) gets off to a fast start in spring and makes a solid, dense plant. It offers late-summer flowers in particularly rich colors from golden yellow to bronze and burgundy red shades.

I can't recommend asters, although they pair so well with heleniums, because they don't hold up too well as cut flowers. An aster "imitator," however, does; it's the boltonia 'Snowbank', useful also for supporting any floppy plants near it.

If you want to keep to pastels, there's a tall, late-blooming, silvery-pink Japanese anemone, *Anemone vitifolia* 'Robustissima'. Purple coneflower is tall enough for the back, too; try letting the seed heads form on one or two of the rigid stems (I had one huge seed head stand through two winters before I cut it down).

Many good perennials of medium height are daisy-flowered, like coreopsis and black-eyed Susans (especially *Rudbeckia* 'Goldsturm'). Others have their flowers in flat-topped clusters; the mustard yellow yarrow 'Coronation Gold' is good for decoration, fresh or dried.

The tall spikes of Kansas gayfeather and the sprays of buttonlike white flowers

KEEPING CUT FLOWERS FRESH

Here are a few practical reminders to help you keep flowers fresh for as long as possible:

- Always cut flowers early in the morning; they will be at their freshest, their stems turgid with water, and blooms refreshed by the night's dew. If early morning is not practical, wait until after sundown.
- Use sharp scissors or flower cutters. Cut as long a stem as you can, because you'll be cutting them again to the desired length when you put them in the containers.
- Strip off any leaves that would be underwater; they'll rot, smell bad, and shorten the life of the flowers.
- Put the cut flowers in a tall container of warm water and stand it in a cool place until you're ready to arrange them. Keep them out of sunshine and away from wind or drafts.

on feverfew liven up a border with their contrast, and are particularly useful in arrangements.

Daylilies suggest themselves as plants that meet the requirements. They have good foliage and beautifully formed flowers of exquisite color but, once indoors in an arrangement, they must be trimmed daily since each blossom lasts only one day.

These are just a few that I have chosen in order to suggest the variety of flower forms that will make bringing them in and having them near you such a joy. A dozen long-stemmed roses or carnations from the florist makes a glamorous gift, but a walk around the garden, clippers in hand, makes you the creator of your own bouquet.

The word "arrange" suggests something more elaborate than I usually lay claim to although, I suppose, we are "arranging" every time we plant our borders. I can't even stuff flowers into a pail without, to some extent, arranging them. So don't be intimidated by all those gorgeous books on flower arranging. Look at them, read them, and enjoy them, but always remember—it's your home and these are your flowers, so go ahead and enjoy yourself! Experiment a little; make them please *your* eye.

*A*NNUALS

What plants could be better suited to a cutting garden? Annuals complete their life cycle in a single growing season, blooming and blooming until they set seed. So, by cutting them for the house, we prolong their blooming time.

Lithium speciosum rubrum *strikes an exotic note in the August border. More commonplace plants like annual poppies and spiderflowers gain importance when silhouetted against the woods.*

The rich crimson of 'Colrain Red' bee balm gives weight to a group of phlox. The lilac pink to the right is 'Franz Schubert'.

The once-blue oat grass, straw-colored by late summer, makes a striking background for dahlias and steel-blue globe thistles in the red border. In the foreground are the flower spikes of lamb's ears (Stachys byzantina).

The 'Galaxy' series of achillea come in subtle colors. This one is 'Salmon Beauty', in front of the old favorite, 'Coronation Gold'.

A low-growing pink baby's breath blooms
for weeks on end if deadheaded.

Border phlox is the very essence of summer.

Rose-red 'Tenor' is the earliest of the summer phloxes in my garden, and especially welcome here because the fluffy, pale-yellow meadowrue will soon be gone, and the light purple catmint (Nepeta sibirica) is not a continuous bloomer. 'Tenor' will hold center stage for two to three months.

Borders like this one need no mulching. The plants are the mulch and they thrive in the moist soil that their leaves keep shaded. Pink snapdragons set out two weeks earlier begin a long season of bloom.

A stroll along the perennial border presents a fresh picture with every step. The gardener can cut a flower and try it for color against others, suggesting a possible rearrangement of the border.

Pink coneflowers offer a bold silhouette. They are strong
enough to stand tall without support. The handsome
ivory-colored coneflower is shorter. Coming down in
height toward the front of the border, a purple balloon
flower is faced down by a small pink allium.

The phlox 'Tenor' is joined by a pink-tasseled burnet (Sanguisorba obtusa) and 'Bright Eyes', a light
pink phlox with a dark eye. 'Moonbeam', the soft yellow threadleaf coreopsis in front, takes the prize
for long bloom.

A long border is an exercise in arranging by form and color. The tall spires of white foxglove in the rear are echoed by the smaller spires of Kniphofia 'Little Maid', in the front. A phlox, 'Leo Schlageter', offers one touch of red to spark this all-pastel border.

To the pale gold of daylilies and the silver of artemisias in the front, foxgloves, a big balloon flower, and tall snapdragons add sparkle with their white flowers.

Lavender wraps around a curve and pulls the border together. A few audacious Johnny-jump-ups appear among the purple spikes.

A stone path and a single stone step lead to a small lawn area fifteen feet square. The edges of the path are softened by sedum and creeping thyme that would be lost on a grass edge.

An indulgence of summer color: The wands of Liatris spicata break up a mass of pink phlox; a purple balloon flower is held up by the strong stems of the deep pink Echinacea 'Bravado', as are the tousled flowers of Monarda 'Croftway Pink' behind them.

Foliage alone would make this composition interesting, with such contrast in form and texture. Color is in one subdued shade. 'Gateway', a German hybrid of our familiar joe-pye weed, is faced down by tall, August-blooming Astilbe taquetii *'Superba'. Biennial* Angelica gigas *is so nearly black in color that it seems to belong to the dark woods in the background.*

Late August in the yellow border. Tiger lilies and a tall yellow coneflower rise between the wall and clumps of Achillea 'Coronation Gold' and the popular rudbeckia 'Goldsturm'. One outrageous touch of orange is offered by a daylily that blooms well into September, and some refreshing white cones from the garlic chives (Allium tuberosum). In the far corner is a trio of lamb's ears, orange pansies, and the tiny, lime-green trumpets of annual Nicotiana langsdorfii.

On a beautiful October day, all jobs are agreeable, even digging dahlia tubers for winter storage.

The pond and its white birches provide background for the red bed. Crimson bee balm and a cherry-red phlox share the spotlight with the annual spider flower Cleome 'Violet Queen'. Globe thistle is in its second flush of leaves and flowers. In the foreground, crimson snapdragon and Gaillardia 'Burgundy' keep the color going through September.

There are annuals and there are annuals. Some, native to warmer parts of the world, are tender. These are usually seeded and raised indoors and not set out until danger of frost is past. At the end of summer, they are the first to be blackened and killed by an early frost. Zinnias, cosmos, and heliotrope are typical of this group.

Fortunately for gardeners in the cooler parts of the country, there are annuals that can take lower temperatures and survive light frost. Some are even hardier; their seeds can lie in the ground all winter and germinate in spring. These are the sturdiest and earliest of all the annuals in the garden, and I consider myself lucky since among them are three of my favorites—love-in-a-mist, bachelor's buttons, and California poppy (many other poppies, too).

I like to seed a few annuals indoors, under lights, but I do less of this each year and rely more on the excellent nurseries in the area. It's a good idea either to place a firm order for the varieties and colors you want or—this should really read "and"—haunt the nursery until you get what your heart desires.

The annuals you want will not all be available at the same time. Get the hardy ones early and plant them out to be growing while you wait for the danger of frost to be past, so that you can make another trip for the tender ones.

I'm a great believer in direct seeding out in the garden. It's not always the neatest-looking planting, but it certainly is natural-looking and gives me the effect I like, that of plants venturing into one another's space (I also grow annuals in rows in the vegetable garden—it's like having my own garden store; I can go and get plants to put in places that need them later in the season).

I sometimes put in a few purchased plants and direct-seed among them. The little plants, being of recognizable size, identify the area. I try not to seed too thickly, but I don't worry about it if it happens. I thin out for the first time when the seedlings are tiny. Later, I can spread them out and find a place for the extras. This has an added advantage; some annuals play themselves out earlier than others, but the plants from the direct seeding will extend the bloom time.

Grow the greatest variety of flower shapes and colors that you can find and have room for. You probably won't be able to plant as closely as in a border designed for mass effect. These cutting-bed annuals are expected to produce top-quality flowers in abundance. Give them room to breathe, watch over them for disease or insect damage, and give them plenty of water in dry weather.

*T*HE "EXTRAS"

I wouldn't hesitate to use any space that was left to grow summer bulbs or tubers, foliage plants, or even house plants that might yield something interesting.

A cutting bed is an excellent place to grow one or two dahlias. I say one or two because these plants make enormous growth and you won't have room for more. They seem like magic plants to me, but certainly nothing I can take credit for. In early spring I buy the tubers in the form and color I want, plant them when the soil warms up, and then stand back.

One thing I can take credit for is lifting and storing them over the winter. The tubers multiply enormously and combined with my spring buying sprees there's danger of outgrowing storage space in the cool part of the basement.

Gray- or silver-leaved plants that are beautiful growing in the border are not always successful when cut. Don't expect good results from 'Silver Mound' or other artemisias with very finely dissected leaves. 'Silver Queen' looks lovely with blues and lavenders, and holds up well in water, but it's a bit rambunctious and you'll need to restrict its growth in a border of this kind.

Many culinary herbs are every bit as decorative as they are tasty. If you want interesting colored foliage, give thought to planting the purple herb *Perilla frutescens*, or the purple-leafed basil. One plant of tricolor sage will yield sprigs of leaves in darkest green, purple, and red. A few dill plants provide lovely lime green flower heads, and the common pot marjoram, cut when the flowers are tight purple buds, contributes filler material for kitchen flowers.

*F*LOWERS INDOORS

I believe I can make flowers look pleasing in almost anything except a container designed to hold them. The phrase "flower vase" has always chilled me. I know that a dozen perfect roses are breathtaking in leaded crystal, but I only have one piece and it's too modest in size for more than a spray of miniature roses.

Don't think you have to go out and buy expensive "vases" in different shapes and sizes. Anything that holds water and is pleasing to look at is a flower container, if you say so, from an inkwell to a casserole. I've enjoyed violets in a teapot, one leathery leaf in the chipped spout; baby's breath in an eggcup, zinnias in a stone mustard jar, and half a meadow's worth of tawny daylilies in an old barrel.

Why do we bring flowers into our homes? At times it's for decoration—a real "flower arrangement" to highlight a painting in the living room, or to grace a hall table. I don't have a hall table (no hall) but I do have one entire fireplace wall of fieldstone, and some days, when the garden is at its height of bloom, I'll gather a huge bunch of flowers and put them in a big pitcher against the fireplace. Indoors, something wonderful happens. I see combinations of colors that were never that close to one another when they grew in the garden, and I've liked some of them well enough to move plants as a result.

That old pitcher was once a ewer, evocative name for the hot-water jug that used to be carried up to freezing bedrooms to encourage morning ablutions. The word "pitcher" still sounds strange to me; the ones I remember from childhood were all "jugs." I used to hear about pitchers, though from my grandparents, who would always say when I came into the room, "Shh! Little pitchers have big ears." I would look at the numerous photographs on the wall and, yes, it was true; some did have big ears.

I fill those big jugs of flowers in the early part of the summer, when the garden overflows with lilacs, then with peonies and delphiniums. Most often, though, for me, it's one flower, with perhaps a bud or a single leaf, in a small container on the desk as I'm working, and by my bed, night and morning. Beautiful and amazing as the mass of flowers may be in the border, one bloom beside you can tell you a lot about itself and bring you to an affectionate understanding of the flower.

One day when it's pouring with rain, or you've broken your leg and can't be out working in the garden (and you're darned if you're going to do any of the things that need doing indoors), take a pencil and draw that one flower you've come to know so well. If there's a paint-box in the house and you can find a brush, experiment. It's not true that only artists can draw and paint—you might be surprised. Surprised hardly describes the reaction of a kindergarten teacher who set a bunch of daisies in front of a young friend of mine, Amy, then five years old, and told her to paint the flowers. Amy did, until every petal dripped with glorious color. Gilding the lily, you might say.

*F*LOWERS FOR CUTTING

*M*AINLY PASTEL COLORS

Annuals

China aster	*Callistephus chinensis*	Pincushion flower	*Scabiosa atropurpurea*
Globe candytuft	*Iberis umbellata*	Pinks	*Dianthus chinensis*
Cosmos	*Cosmos bipinnatus*	Sweet william	*D. barbatus* (biennial)
Larkspur	*Consolida ambigua*	Snapdragon	*Antirrhinum majus*
Petunia	*Petunia*	Tobacco flower	*Nicotiana alata*

Perennials

Baby's breath	*Gypsophila paniculata*	Delphinium	*Delphinium elatum*
Balloon flower	*Playtcodon grandiflorus*	Japanese anemone	*Anemone × hybrida*
Columbine	*Aquilegia* hybrids	Peony	*Paeonia lactiflora*
Coneflower	*Echinacea purpurea*	Sea lavender	*Limonium latifolium*
Coralbells	*Heuchera* hybrids	Yarrow	*Achillea* hybrids

"*H*OT" COLORS—YELLOW, ORANGE, RED

Annuals

Blanketflower	*Gaillardia pulchella*	Pot marigold	*Calendula officinalis*
Cosmos (yellow)	*Cosmos sulphureus*	Sunflower	*Helianthus annuus* ('Autumn Beauty' and 'Italian White')
Gloriosa daisy	*Rudbeckia*		
Marigold	*Tagetes erecta*	Tickseed	*Coreopsis tinctoria*
Mexican sunflower	*Tithonia rotundifolia*	Zinnia	*Zinnia elegans*

Perennials

Black-eyed Susan	*Rudbeckia hirta*	Helen's flower (sneezeweed)	*Helenium autumnale*
Daylily	*Hemerocallis × hybrida*		
False sunflower	*Heliopsis* 'Summer Sun'	Yarrow	*Achillea* 'Moonshine', A. 'Coronation Gold'
Goldenrod	*Solidago* 'Golden Fleece'		

USEFUL WHITES

Annual

Baby's breath   *Gypsophila elegans*

Perennials

Coneflower	*Echinacea* 'White Swan'	Spike speedwell	*Veronica* 'Icicle'
	E. 'White Lustre'	Yarrow	*Achillea* 'The Pearl'
Garlic chive	*Allium tuberosum*		

PURPLES, BLUES

Annuals

Bachelor's buttons	*Centaurea cyanus*	Verbena	*Verbena* 'Amethyst'
Mealycup sage	*Salvia farinacea* 'Victoria'	Kansas gayfeather	*Liatris spicata*
Love-in-a-mist	*Nigella damascena* 'Miss Jekyll'	Russian sage	*Perovskia atriplicifolia*

FOLIAGE, SEEDHEADS

Annuals

Flame nettle	*Coleus*	Perilla	*Perilla frutescens*
Bells of Ireland	*Moluccella laevis*	Drumstick	*Scabiosa stellata* (seed heads)

Perennials

Heuchera	*Heuchera* 'Palace Purple' (leaves)	Silver queen	*Artemisia* 'Silver Queen'
Plantain lily	*Hosta* hybrids	Variegated sage	*Salvia tricolor*

TENDER BULBS, CORMS, TUBERS

Dahlias (many colors and flower forms)
Gladiolus (variety of colors and sizes)
Acidanthera (exotic, heavily fragrant, white)

....

CHAPTER 13

PREPARING FOR WINTER

When I first began to garden at Heath we were there for the summer and weekends only. I remember those wrenching Sunday departures in September and October, and the weekly gamble on whether there would be a killing frost before our return on Friday.

Back then I had a fair-sized vegetable garden, and the anxiety about tomatoes and late zucchini added to the general angst about the flower garden. Perhaps, I reasoned, I'd get a few more flowers; an anemone still in bud might bloom, some of the green tomatoes might get a little closer to red. So I'd leave everything growing and head for five days of worry in the city. Once in a while the gamble paid off and I won another week or two of flowers and produce, but for the most part I was the loser, returning to mounds of blackened plants.

When I found myself unable to face the weekly decision-making any longer, I embarked on another ridiculous course of action. Everything that gave as much as a hint of bud or fruit had to be packed into the station wagon and taken to the city. It wasn't just our garden harvest. There were several dozen house plants to be returned to my school classroom, and often there were last-minute gifts of vegetables from neighbors, themselves overburdened with produce. ("No, thanks" was not in my vocabulary then.)

The end came one Sunday night at a gas station on the way home. Our dog took exception to a small yapping terrier in a car parked alongside ours, and—the better to see the enemy—jumped into the collection of boxes and baskets in the back of our car. The food processing effect of a 120-pound German shepherd on a basket of Concord grapes is impossible to describe. Back at the apartment we unpacked the car and dripped our purple way across the black-and-white tiled lobby. I knew I didn't want any more of these desperate attempts to hold on to summer.

I had once been shocked to hear a colleague at school, another weekend gardener, say she couldn't wait for a frost to come and put an end to it all. I realized that "gardeners' greed"—wanting more, more, more, and being unwilling to relinquish anything—was at the root of my trouble. It was a relief when I learned to let go, and fall has not been such a threat to me since.

The first light frost takes only the most tender of the annual flowers; heliotrope and cosmos are the first to go. The next frost, often a little sharper, will finish off perilla and any basil plants. It also browns the petals of Japanese anemone and the flower spikes on the late snakeroot. Some years, the first frost is *the* frost, with temperatures dropping into the low twenties and killing almost all the annuals in one onslaught. I like it better when frost kills annuals a few at a time because the cleanup is so much easier done in stages.

The last flowers left are the tough ones, like bachelor's buttons, calendulas, and snapdragons, and I'm so grateful for them at this winding down of the year. Snapdragons, especially, are marvelous because as the weather turns colder they respond by getting stronger and bushier, with leaves of shiny, lustrous quality. As I write the word snapdragon the sharp, spicy smell of the flowers comes into the room. They are usually grown as annuals in the cooler parts of this country, but

Garden cleanup is much easier done in stages. Tender annuals like cosmos, cleome, and heliotrope are the first to be nipped by frost, and can be cleared out while perennials remain in bloom.

Cannas are dug from the pond's edge; they will winter over in the bucket in a cool basement without further attention.

with a heavy mulch it's sometimes possible to bring them through the winter.

When the clocks are turned back, things get harder for gardeners, but especially for part-time gardeners. A child complained once that "it gets late earlier," and I know what he meant. There's no daylight left by the time people get home from work, and it takes iron resolve to get out in the garden before leaving in the morning. Every minute is valuable and if some part of the cleanup is done after each early frost the whole job is made more manageable. Besides, the spaces left by these annuals can be forked over and enriched. If it's early enough in the fall, they can be used for transplanted biennials or perennials.

Every year, that first frost galvanizes me into action—no point pretending any longer—it's time to fast forward and get a move on with preparation for winter. Never mind if winter isn't official until a few days before Christmas; to me, it begins when the ground freezes and gardening has to stop (except in the mind, where some of the best gardening flourishes all winter long).

I sometimes fear that one day I'll be called to account for the gap between precept and example in some of my gardening. I really mean it when I say that one should grow the plants that are right for the zone one gardens in. One should not have to fuss over and cosset temperamental plants that are not really temperamental at all, but are simply being grown in the wrong climate. Yet, in spite of this, I grow the chocolate cosmos (*Cosmos atrosanguineus*)—as an annual, let me say, for this plant is native to Mexico and not hardy north of Zone 7 here.

I maintain stoutly that mine is a garden where "shape up or ship out" is the order of the day, and that plants should be able to take care of themselves over winter. Nevertheless, I sometimes sneak back up to the garden after we've left for the winter and put a mulch of pine needles on such borderline hardy plants as the 'Little Maid' poker plants and the broom plant (*Cytisus praecox*).

I think you, the reader, will have to distinguish the "one should"'s from the "what I do"'s, and make your own decision. Very often it comes down to how much time you have. Fall weather is unpredictable; a lingering, rainy October with no frost can keep everything growing so vigorously that you hate to cut it down, and can make the soil so wet that you can't get on it to work.

As soon as conditions permit, however, there are a number of things you should do that will be good for the garden in winter and good for you in spring, when everything needs doing at once. You will note that I begin the list with something *not* to do, and this is very important:

- **Do Not Mulch Yet.** If you do, the mice will see it as a homemaking opportunity; you must wait until the ground is frozen. This timing is awkward, especially if heavy snow falls before the ground freezes. While you're waiting for this, you can be gathering your mulching materials but do keep them protected from weather. I've found that even the pine needles I use freeze together if they get wet and are very hard to apply as a mulch.
- While the soil is still soft and it's possible to push them in, put markers next to plants that are very late to show in spring, like balloon flower and butterfly weed, for instance. This will help you avoid digging into it inadvertently in spring. If you don't trust labels and markers to stay where you put them (and they do move in the most magical way over winter), mark the position of plants on a rudimentary chart of the border.
- Keep raking fallen leaves off the lawn. Compost some and push others into and around any shrub plantings. Make the final mowing of the lawn quite close, at about two to three inches. When heavy snows lie on grass over winter unsightly snow mold can develop.
- Cut twiggy branches for use as plant supports next spring. If they are cut

now they'll be dead and unlikely to root when you use them. I could cite sad personal experience in support of this advice.

- If the fall is dry, water any new transplants.
- Pick up and either save for burning or bag as trash all foliage of peonies and bearded iris, and any fallen rose leaves afflicted with leaf spot.
- Rough-dig any new areas you want for spring planting, and leave them open for frost to break down the clumps of earth. The exposure to cold will help to reduce the insect population.
- If you plan to lime any part of your garden, fall is a good time to do it (see *Working with the Soil,* page 48).
- Once there has been a freeze cut all perennials down to the ground and add them to the compost pile (annuals will already have been put on the compost).
- Certain annuals do much better from a late fall or winter sowing than from the more usual spring sowing. Annual poppies, bachelor's buttons, and larkspur respond well to this. Sprinkle the seeds on the ground but don't bother to cover them; they'll settle themselves.
- Once the soil is frozen, you can mulch. This will be particularly important for plants that went into the ground this season and are facing their first winter. The thing to understand is that the purpose of mulching is not to keep plants warm but to keep the ground at a consistently low temperature. This prevents their being heaved out of the ground as it alternately freezes and thaws. I've had good results by placing flat stones around the base of the plant as a mulch; their weight holds the soil down around the roots.

At this time of year there will be glorious days that make it a pleasure to be out working on these jobs but there will also be days, most likely in November, when you question the desirability of having a garden at all. You know what I mean—awful weather that sits about in heaps, sunless, leaden days, bone-chilling cold, and, for good measure, a rotten wind blowing sleet at you sideways. Except for raking and digging, which keeps you warm, at least, most of these jobs will be horrible. Give up.

Go inside and have a nice cup of tea or better still, make a pot of tea and invite a garden friend. Compare notes on the season now ended and make a few plans for next year. Tomorrow will be better.

In the Garden

....

The dictionary would have us believe that a garden is "a plot of land used for the cultivation of flowers, vegetables, or fruit." Even when it improves a little in the second definition—"grounds adorned with flowers, shrubs, and trees for public enjoyment"—it seems to me to miss the mark.

Gardens are for people. They are places to imagine, to own, to work in, sometimes to take refuge in. When the whole world seems too big for us, and eludes our grasp, we can simplify it by making a small one for ourselves. Perhaps "garden" is an idea. If so, the possibilities are endless.

Do you remember making a garden when you were very young? I've watched so many children set about doing it and I notice that plants don't seem to be their priority. First they establish what is theirs and set their seal on it by marking the boundaries with sticks or stones. Without exception, the children I know made small gardens; I have never known a child want to make a large one. Perhaps half the charm lies in miniaturization. Even as adults we like to peer into dollhouses, to become for a moment an Alice or a Gulliver.

I was five when I made a garden. It was in a corner of a dusty, overgrown backyard in London. I surrounded a little patch of ground (it couldn't have been more than two feet square) with stones. Then I asked for a "Beware of the Dog" sign (every house in the street had one). Some unfeeling adult pointed out that we didn't have a dog, and I had to settle for "Keep Out." I don't remember any planting, although I do remember picking dandelions and wild woodbine, and arranging the flower heads in a circle. Ownership, obviously, counted for a lot.

Children, asked what they would like in the way of a garden, are quite clear: "it's all your own"; "a place to hide"; "not too much grass"; "no places you mustn't go"; "with big rocks to sit on." As a designer of children's games put it, "imaginary games don't fit in neat rows."

While there may very well be gardeners who need to exert rigid control over their plants, and others whose chief interest is in making a showpiece to display to others, there are many, many more whose pleasure it is simply to watch things grow and whose happiness comes from just being in the garden.

It's the *being in it,* after all, that counts, that makes gardening the absorbing thing it is. No matter how beautiful a painting may be, it is to be looked at; it cannot be entered. Most sculpture, too, rarely invites entry. Perhaps gardens are closer to architecture. Wonderful as the prospect of castle or cathedral may be, the excitement is in being inside it and feeling part of the space it encloses.

Few gardens have the grandeur of cathedrals. Often small, they are creations of their owner—expressions of faith and conviction. Whether it's a marble nymph gazing down a hornbeam allée or a plaster gnome on a toadstool; romantic, deep flower borders or a bed of vivid annuals in a little front garden—that's somebody's idea out there. We must assume that each in its way is pleasing to the owner, or the whole thing's for naught.

> So, high road or low road, there we are—
> lucky gardeners all, in our private Edens,
> looking, marveling, with all our senses engaged.
> We are gardening.

". . . in our private Edens . . ."

To purchase a copy of Elsa Bakalar's forty-minute instructional videotape, *Portrait of a Gardener*, please call 1-800-624-2323 or write to National Treasures Productions, Box 2284, South Burlington, VT 05407-2284.

The cost of the tape is $24.95 plus shipping and handling.

A SELECT LIST OF MAIL-ORDER SOURCES
FOR PERENNIAL PLANTS

. . . .

B&D Lilies
330 P Street
Port Townsend, WA 98368
(summer lily bulbs)

Kurt Bluemel
2740 Greene Lane
Baldwin, MD 21013
(wide selection ornamental grasses)

Bluestone Perennials
7211 Middle Ridge Road
Madison, OH 44057
(small first-year plants)

Busse Gardens
Rte 2 Box 238
Cokato, MN 55321

Canyon Creek Nursery
3527 Dry Creek Road
Oroville, CA 95965
(many interesting imports)

Crownsville Nursery
P.O.B. 797
Crownsville, MD 21032

Forever Green Farm
70 New Gloucester Road
North Yarmouth, ME 04097
(old roses and David Austin roses)

Holbrook Farm & Nursery
Rte 2 Box 223B
Fletcher, NC 28732

Klehm Nursery
Rte 5 Box 197
South Barrington, IL 60010
(extensive peony list)

Milaeger's Gardens
4838 Douglas Ave.
Racine, WI 53402-2498

Sandy Mush Herb Nursery
Rte 2
Surrett Cove Road
Leicester, NC 28748

Andre Viette Farm & Nursery
Rte 1 Box 16
Fishersville, VA 22939

Wayside Gardens
Hodges, SC 29695-0001

White Flower Farm
Litchfield, CT 06759-0050

$\mathcal{A}$ SHORT READING LIST

. . . .

Bubel, Nancy. *The New Seed-Starters Handbook* (Emmaus, PA: Rodale Press, 1988).

Charlesworth, Geoffrey B. *The Opinionated Gardener* (Boston: David Godine, 1988).

Druse, Ken. *The Natural Garden* (New York: Clarkson Potter, Inc., 1989).

Glattstein, Judy. *Garden Design with Foliage* (Pownal, VT: Storey Communications, 1991).

Harper, Pamela J. *Designing with Perennials* (New York: Macmillan Publishing Co., Inc., 1991).

Hobhouse, Penelope. *Color in Your Garden* (Boston: Little, Brown, 1985).

Martin, Laura C. *The Wildflower Meadow Book* (Charlotte, NC: Fast & McMillan Publishers, Inc., 1986).

McGourty, Frederick. *The Perennial Garden* (Boston: Houghton Mifflin Co., 1989).

Morse, Harriet K. *Gardening in the Shade* (Beaverton, OR: Timber Press, 1982).

Schenk, George. *The Complete Shade Gardener* (Boston: Houghton Mifflin Co., 1985).

Sheldon, Elizabeth. *A Proper Garden* (Harrisburg, PA: Stackpole Books, 1989).

Wilder, Louise Beebe. *Color in My Garden* (New York: Atlantic Monthly Press, 1990 [first published in 1918 by Doubleday, Page & Co.]).

For Reference

Armitage, Allan M. *Herbaceous Perennial Plants* (Athens, GA: Varsity Press, Inc., 1989).

Barton, Barbara. *Gardening by Mail* (Boston: Houghton Mifflin Co., 1990). (A useful source book listing nurseries, plant societies, publications, libraries, etc.)

Clausen, Ruth Rogers and Nicolas H. Ekstrom. *Perennials for American Gardens* (New York: Random House, 1989).

Taylor's Guides. *Taylor's Guide to Perennials* (Boston: Houghton Mifflin Co., 1986). (One of a series including *Annuals, Shrubs, Garden Design,* and many others.)

Wyman, Donald. *Wyman's Garden Encyclopedia* (New York: Macmillan Publishing Co., Inc., 1986).

INDEX

. . . .

Page numbers in *italics* refer to illustrations and border designs.